We cultivate literature on a little oatmeal...

An Introduction to Edinburgh as the first UNESCO City of Literature

'We cultivate literature on a little oatmeal...' the Rev Sydney Smith's wittily proposed motto for The Edinburgh Review, March 1802.

Edinburgh UNESCO City of Literature Trust

This edition published in 2005 by
Edinburgh UNESCO City of Literature Trust
137 Dundee Street, Edinburgh EH11 1BG
E: edinburgh@cityofliterature.com W: www.cityofliterature.com

British Library Cataloguing in Publication Data
A record for this book is available from the British Library

ISBN 0-954-86572-3

Design by Redpath, www.redpath.co.uk

Printed and bound by OZGraf S.A. Olsztyn, Poland, EU
Production Management by **POLSKABOOK**, Warsaw, Poland, EU

EUCL Trust acknowledges the support of the Scottish Arts Council and
The Scottish Executive in the production of this publication.

Contents

Forewords

Dugald Stewart monument at night with the cityscape below

From the Office of the First Minister

Edinburgh's literary heritage is legendary. Scotland's first printing press was built in Edinburgh in 1507, and gave rise to a publishing industry which still flourishes today.

During the Enlightenment, when it was said that visitors to Edinburgh could meet 50 men of genius within a few minutes simply by standing at the city's Mercat Cross, writers such as David Hume and Adam Smith changed not only Scotland, but the world, forever.

And the city has been home to some of the world's best loved poets and novelists. Robert Burns wrote some of his best work during his time in Scotland's capital, as did Robert Louis Stevenson. And today, Edinburgh's J.K. Rowling entrances millions of children around the world with her wonderful novels. Arthur Conan Doyle, born in the New Town, wrote one of the most famous crime fiction books ever written, whilst today, Ian Rankin is renowned for his Rebus crime thrillers set in and around the City.

The pursuit of knowledge has always been central to Scottish life, and in 1890 Edinburgh's first free public library opened. Today there are over 100 libraries in the city, ranging from the world-famous National Library of Scotland to small community libraries which make sure that literature is available to all, regardless of where they live.

The written word informs and entertains people across the globe. For centuries, Edinburgh has been among the leading centres for publishing, writing and libraries. I am very pleased to support Edinburgh's ambition to be recognised as a UNESCO City of Literature.

Jack McConnell, First Minister

From the Lord Provost

Lesley Hinds, Lord Provost

Edinburgh is a city which wears many hats – Scotland's capital, home of the Scottish Parliament, the Festival City, a financial centre, and, since 1995, the Old and New Towns have been recognised as a World Heritage Site. But this is also a city built on books – a walk down the Royal Mile quickly establishes the central role books have played, and continue to play, from the founding of the *Encyclopaedia Britannica* in Anchor Close, the establishment of Scotland's first lending library and the printing presses of the Enlightenment, the Writers' Museum and Makar's Court, to the development of a new Literature Quarter housing Scotland's literature organisations and publishers who are continuing to make headlines in the 21st century. The city has provided inspiration for many writers over the centuries, and presently is home to some of the leading writers in the world. And every August the city, ablaze with festivals, welcomes over 500 writers from all corners of the globe to the biggest and best known literature event, the Edinburgh International Book Festival.

The award of this prestigious title would be a start, rather an end in itself. In putting itself forward for this designation, the City of Edinburgh commits itself to re-emphasise the central role of literature in the lives of all its citizens. Building upon the existing foundation of programmes such as Books for Babies, we will work to foster creativity, develop readership and improve literacy from the earliest years, across all ages and communities. We also undertake to honour our literary heritage, and promote our thriving contemporary literature scene. Finally, the designation will assist us to forge links and partnerships with other great literature cities of the world.

From J.K. Rowling

Edinburgh has been my home since 1994. It was the place that Harry Potter took shape; as has been well-documented, I used to sit in the Old Town's cafes scribbling as my young daughter slept in her pushchair next to me. And I nervously posted off the manuscript for *Harry Potter and the Philosopher's Stone* from a post box in Leith.

All the books in the series so far have been created largely in Edinburgh. My base in Scotland has given me many advantages and inspirations as the series has developed, and as I've found myself more and more in the public eye. I'm proud to be known as a Scottish writer, albeit by adoption – although my Scottish ancestors would have been even prouder to have heard me described as such, I think.

So I have personal reasons for finding the city creatively inspirational. But it's also impossible to live in Edinburgh without sensing its literary heritage everywhere. It seems eminently sensible to me to recognise this, along with the contemporary literary life here, with a permanent title that can inspire and inform other places around the world.

J.K. Rowling, Author

Preface

Edinburgh already is a world city of literature. Its great heritage of the book and its contemporary literary life define it as a cultural capital for the ages. The idea of a formal designation came about because four book lovers thought that Edinburgh, and indeed, Scotland, should take on responsibility for the future development of a literary culture that has distinguished and enlightened our country's past.

We want to share the literary culture of our capital city with the world. Edinburgh is not proposed as *the* UNESCO City of Literature but one of many, we hope. The idea is not about competition but about aspiration and partnership.

It is not going too far to say that here in Scotland's great capital city there are today all the signs and legacies of a culture of writing, reading and publishing that have enhanced Western civilisation. There is genius in the culture of Edinburgh but there is also a tradition of great geniality and conviviality. This is a scholarly place but it is also a place of festivity and cultural clamour. In that spirit, four of us shaped a designation that confers upon Edinburgh the responsibility of sharing its culture. Scottish Arts Council backed the idea from the start, and enthusiasm for the idea swiftly grew among the literature community of the city.

Our idea in offering this title, UNESCO City of Literature, is for its continuing and proliferating use across the globe. It is not intended to be an exclusive mark for Edinburgh but rather a mantle to don for those whose past merits it and whose ambition is up to it.

To be a "UNESCO City of Literature" indicates four things:

- A city should have, like Edinburgh, historic distinction in some area – or areas – of literary activity whether that be writing, publishing, selling, teaching, lending or celebrating literature.
- The designation also indicates an open contemporary culture of writing, reading, learning and publishing.
- A UNESCO City of Literature must have ambitions to extend its literary culture to the next generation at home and to other cities in a global partnership. It will wish to invest in its youth, ensuring universal literacy, promoting the interests of writers, offering literature for sale freely, building the resource of books and ensuring the freedom to write, publish, sell and read books of all sorts and from all sources.

The fourth characteristic of UNESCO Cities of Literature is that they operate in partnerships: they are partners in the future of the culture of the book.

- A UNESCO City of Literature is one that accepts the responsibility to develop and share literary culture across the globe, disseminating writing, allowing no barriers of language, and determining year by year to fulfil its task.

The idea of Cities of Literature will find enthusiasts worldwide. We now announce that Edinburgh, capital of Scotland, is ready to welcome partners in developing a worldwide chain of cities of literature.

This document is our exuberant presentation of the Edinburgh of the book, its history, its vibrant contemporary culture and its literary ambitions. This is not a set of criteria for other cities to emulate. It is a portrait of our city and it is meant to thrill you wherever you are in the world and lure you here and inspire your own journey through literature, words and ideas.

James Boyle.

Jenny Brown

Lorraine Fannin

Catherine Lockerbie

James Boyle, Jenny Brown, Lorraine Fannin, Catherine Lockerbie.

We wish to acknowledge the support and funding of the Scottish Executive and Scottish Arts Council, and of Scottish Publishers Association and Edinburgh International Book Festival.

Edinburgh, Summer 2004.

Chapter 1. Scotland's contribution to world literature

Chapter 1
Scotland's contribution to world literature

Scottish literature defines the cultural image of Scotland for many people around the world. Edinburgh-based writers have been inspired to create world renowned and lasting literary characters such as Peter Pan and Sherlock Holmes, and authored famous books such as *Dr Jekyll and Mr Hyde* and *Treasure Island*. Over the centuries, Edinburgh-based writers have pioneered the popular novel, the historical novel, the psychological thriller and the detective genre and the work of Scotland's leading writers, poets and playwrights has been translated into many languages for an international audience.

Fantasy, satire, traditionally-built ladies and Porno: writers in Scotland today

Ian Rankin is the UK's best selling crime writer and is renowned for his series of novels featuring Inspector John Rebus, set in contemporary Edinburgh. He was awarded an OBE for literature in 2002, and in 2004 was awarded an Edgar by the USA.

'I started writing novels while an undergraduate student, in an attempt to make sense of the city of Edinburgh, using a detective as my protagonist. Each book hopefully adds another piece to the jigsaw that is modern Scotland, asking questions about the nation's politics, economy, psyche and history…and perhaps pointing towards its possible future.'

Springtime in Edinburgh. A freezing wind, and ne that black farce of a wind. Making everyone walk like mi on rid-nipped cheeks. And throughout it all, that slightly s

2.

3.   4.

Irvine Welsh has been a cult figure within the writing world since the 1990s. The seismic impact of *Trainspotting* – a searing anatomy of urban dysfunction and a dispossessed chemical generation – fundamentally altered the landscape and profile of Scottish fiction, and created for it a completely new readership. As a film, *Trainspotting* was a box-office success worldwide. Welsh's books combine comedy, drama and the gritty side of Edinburgh to create international bestsellers. Other Welsh novels have been brought to the screen, including *The Acid House*. Welsh's latest title, a sequel to *Trainspotting* called *Porno*, is also being released as a film.

Candia McWilliam also chooses darker subject matter in her writing. Born in Edinburgh, she is an acclaimed contemporary novelist and short story writer. Her three novels include *Debatable Land*, set in Edinburgh and the South Seas. Kate Atkinson is one of the bestselling fiction writers in the UK. Her first novel *Behind the Scenes at the Museum* won the overall Whitbread Book of the Year. She has since published three novels, a book of short stories and two plays for the Traverse Theatre in Edinburgh.

Iain Banks is one of the most inventive novelists of his generation and one of Britain's best selling authors. Iain Banks' debut novel *The Wasp Factory*, about a troubled teenager, was an international bestseller and has sold a million copies.

1. Peter Pan illustrated by Mabel Lucie Atwell
2. Iain Banks reading at the Edinburgh International Book Festival
3. Candia McWilliam, acclaimed contemporary author
4. Irvine Welsh, as depicted by illustrator Iain McIntosh

rizontal rain. Ah, the Edinburgh wind, that joke of a wind, sts, making eyes water and then drying the tears to a crust sty smell in the air, the smell of not-so-distant breweries.

1.   2.   3.   4.   5.

1. Masthead illustration by Iain McIntosh for the *Scotsman* serialisation of the novel *44 Scotland Street*
2. The first in the series of the *No. 1 Ladies' Detective Agency* novels by McCall Smith
3. Alexander McCall Smith
4. Traverse poster for *Perfect Days*, by Liz Lochhead
5. Edwin Morgan, Scotland's first Poet Laureate. Detail from Poets' Pub painting by Alexander Moffat

His 1992 novel *The Crow Road* was adapted for television. Under his alter ego, Iain M. Banks, he has produced an equally popular and acclaimed series of science fiction novels.

It's a long journey in both geography and the mind from Edinburgh to the dustiness of Botswana. Yet this is the setting chosen for the stories of one of Edinburgh's most captivating authors, Alexander McCall Smith. Born in Zimbabwe and educated there and in Scotland, he now makes his home in Edinburgh where he is Professor of Medical Law at the University of Edinburgh. His series of stories based around the investigations and musings of Botswana's only lady detective have charmed audiences worldwide and are especially popular in the USA. As well as writing *The No. 1 Ladies' Detective Agency* series, McCall Smith has authored specialist titles such as *Forensic Aspects of Sleep* and *The Criminal Law of Botswana* as well as novels for children including *The Perfect Hamburger*. 2004 will see the start of a new series of novels set in Edinburgh, the first of which has already been serialised in the *Scotsman* newspaper.

Liz Lochhead is one of Scotland's foremost contemporary playwrights and poets, and was a Writer in Residence at Edinburgh University in the eighties. Her best known plays include *Mary Queen of Scots Had her Head Chopped Off*, *Dracula*, and *Perfect Days*. Her strong interest in French literature has led to translations into Scots of Moliere's *Tartuffe* and *Les Misanthropes*.

Mma Ramotswe had a DETECTIVE AGENCY in AFRICA, at the foot of K
and an old typewriter. Then there was a TEAPOT, in which Mma Ramot
And THREE MUGS – one for HERSELF, one for her SECRETARY, and

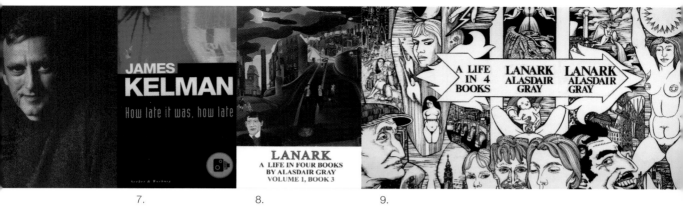

7.   8.   9.

James Kelman is one of Scotland's most radical and influential authors whose ground-breaking narrative techniques and intensity of voice and style have drawn comparisons with Kafka, Joyce, and Beckett. His *How Late It Was, How Late* was a controversial choice as winner of the Booker Prize for Fiction. Based in Glasgow, Kelman is a writer of considerable substance and range: he also writes screenplays and plays for radio and theatre.

Since the publication of his debut epic novel *Lanark: A Life in Four Books* in 1981, Alasdair Gray has been recognised as one of the most innovative figures in contemporary literature and culture. Blending satire and tragedy, realism and fantasy, his work spurred a renaissance in Scottish literature and foreshadowed a new wave of outstanding Scottish writing. Gray is highly acclaimed around the world, including the USA where he has been described as 'one of the most important living writers in English'.

Scotland's first Poet Laureate Edwin Morgan is the country's most popular contemporary poet. Morgan established himself as a major poet with the publication of *The Second Life*. His *Poems of Thirty Years* runs to over 400 pages, and his verse is taught extensively in Scottish schools. Morgan is also a dramatist and literary translator from German, Italian, Spanish and Russian.

6. James Kelman, whose writing has been compared with Kafka, Joyce and Beckett
7. *How Late it Was, How Late,* winner of the Booker Prize for Fiction
8. Cover image of *Lanark: A Life in Four Books*
9. Black and white etching of *Lanark: A Life in Four Books* by Alasdair Gray

. These were its assets: a tiny van, two desks, two chairs, a telephone, he ONLY LADY DETECTIVE in Botswana – brewed RED BUSH TEA. the CLIENT. What else does a detective agency really need?

1.　　　　　　　　　　　　2.　　　　　　　　3.

From la crème de la crème to Sunset Song: twentieth-century novelists

One of the world's leading contemporary novelists in English and the author of one of Scotland's greatest novels, Muriel Spark (b.1918), was born and brought up in Edinburgh and remains closely associated with the city. Her novel *The Prime of Miss Jean Brodie* stands as one of the great pieces of Scottish literature. Set in Edinburgh and modelled on Spark's former school, James Gillespie's High School for Girls, it is filled with allusions to the city's topography, history, character and literary past. The novel's central character, the schoolmistress Jean Brodie, leads a double life. 'An Edinburgh spinster of the deepest dye', she also has liberal views ahead of her time. Spark's novels have been made into films, translated into many languages and won her several international literary awards. She has commented that 'Edinburgh had an effect on my mind, my prose style and my ways of thought'.

Dorothy Dunnett's (1923-2001) significant contribution to Scottish literature led to her award of an OBE for Services to Literature. Dunnett is best known as the author of two historical series: the six-volume *Lymond Chronicles* and *The House of Niccolò*, which won her one of the largest and most devoted readerships of any Scottish writer. Her work inspires worldwide discussion and acclaim through websites, chatrooms, a magazine and international gatherings.

Miss Brodie ushered the girls from the music room a If I were to receive a **proposal** of marriage tomorrow from to you in my prime. Form a single file, now, and walk with yo

5.   6.   7.   8.

Lewis Grassic Gibbon (1901-1935) was born James Leslie Mitchell in the Scottish town of Auchterless but soon moved to the Mearns, the rural Scotland he was to make famous in his great trilogy *A Scots Quair,* consisting of three novels, *Sunset Song, Cloud Howe* and *Grey Granite.*

Many of his novels were autobiographical and celebrated the Scotland that Gibbon had known in his youth before the ravages of the First World War. His later Scottish novels moved away from nostalgia and depicted the industrial Scotland of his day. Gibbon used a lyrical and expressive Scots language that was easily understood by non-Scots readers. The adaptation of his books for television brought him before international audiences in America and Canada, and his work was translated into a number of different languages.

Neil M. Gunn (1891-1973) also wrote of the Scotland he knew. Born on the northernmost shores of Scotland into a family of fishermen, he was to become one of Scotland's most celebrated writers.

Gunn's short stories published throughout the 1920s are closely identified with the Scottish Renaissance spearheaded by Hugh MacDiarmid. His early novels *Grey Coast* and *The Lost Glen* describe the effect of the economic stagnation in the Scottish Highlands during the 1920s, while the history of the area is brought to life in *Sun Circle, Butcher's Broom* and *The Silver Darlings.* Gunn's writing presents an important depiction of life in the Highlands of Scotland and quickly won an international reputation, particularly in Europe.

4. Muriel Spark, one of the world's leading contemporary novelists
5. Neil M. Gunn, celebrated writer from Caithness
6. *Sunset Song*, by Lewis Grassic Gibbon
7. *Highland River* by Neil M. Gunn
8. *The Serpent* by Neil M. Gunn

hering them about her, said "You girls are my **vocation.** rd Lyon King-of-Arms I would **decline** it. I am dedicated ads up, up like Sybil Thorndyke, a woman of noble mien."

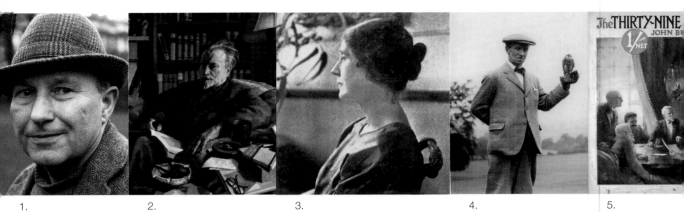

1.   2.   3.   4.   5.

1. Robert Garioch, poet
2. Compton Mackenzie, author of *Whisky Galore*
3. Catherine Carswell, respected and widely published journalist and novelist
4. John Buchan, barrister, politician, statesman and novelist
5. Artwork for the cover of the one-shilling 'bookstall' edition of *The Thirty-Nine Steps*, published by William Blackwood

Catherine Carswell (1879-1946) was a respected and widely published female journalist of her time. She was encouraged by her friend D.H. Lawrence to write her first novel, *Open the Door!*, notable for its frank treatment of independence and sexuality in its heroine. She also wrote a groundbreaking biography of Robert Burns. The noted feminist writer Rebecca West (1892-1983) was educated in Edinburgh. Her work includes the novel *The Birds Fall Down* and her two-volume study of the Yugoslav nation *Black Lamb and Grey Falcon*.

A novelist who chose Edinburgh as his home for the last 40 years of his life, Compton Mackenzie (1883-1972) authored *Whisky Galore*, a fictional account of the sinking of a ship laden with whisky off the Scottish Island of Eriskay. A finely observed comedy of Scottish life, it was made into a film, as was Mackenzie's novel *Rockets Galore*.

John Buchan (1875-1940), was not only a barrister, politician and statesman, but also a successful novelist most acclaimed for his adventure stories. The best loved of these involve his hero Richard Hannay: *The Thirty-Nine Steps*, *Greenmantle*, *Mr Standfast* and *The Island of Sheep*. *The Thirty-Nine Steps* has spawned a number of film and television adaptations – this novel alone has been translated into many languages including Arabic, Burmese, Chinese, Estonian, Japanese, Korean, Romanian, Serbo-Croat and Thai.

Where is Scudder's book?" I cried to Sir Walter, "Quick, man and gave it to me. I found the place. THIRTY-NINE STEPS I re was at 10.17p.m. The admiralty man was looking at me as if

7.   8.   9.

Regard for the thistle: twentieth-century poets and playwrights

Sorley MacLean (1911-1996) was responsible for the revival of the Gaelic poetic tradition. His collection of poems *Dàin do Eimhir agus Dain Eile* was the first published collection of Gaelic verse in the modern idiom, and had a profound influence on contemporary Gaelic poetry, and beyond. Speaking with a new voice and of the modern age, MacLean's poetry retained the traditional elegance of the Gaelic tongue while reviving the language for the modern era. His work is seen as an essential bridge between classic Gaelic poetry and the future use of the language in literature.

His contemporary, Iain Crichton Smith (1928-1998) (or Iain Mac a' Ghobhainn), wrote in both Gaelic and English, to produce world-class poetry, short stories, novels, plays and radio drama.

Hugh MacDiarmid (1892-1978) used the Scots tongue in his work to profound impact. His work ranged widely in form and intensity, from hauntingly beautiful to raw language; *A Drunk Man Looks at The Thistle* is generally considered his finest work. Robert Garioch (1909-1981) also made a conscious effort to preserve the Scots language and felt a particular affinity with his predecessor Robert Fergusson.

The two contrasting styles of Sydney Goodsir Smith and Norman MacCaig add to this roll call of excellence. The first – distinctive, vibrant and often bawdy, the latter – provocative, rich and intellectual. All have been affected by Edinburgh. All have left their mark.

6. Sorley MacLean, responsible for the revival of the Gaelic tradition
7. Norman MacCaig, Hugh MacDiarmid, Sorley MacLean, Iain Crichton Smith, George Mackay Brown, Sydney Goodsir Smith, Edwin Morgan, Robert Garioch drinking in the Poets' Pub
8. Hugh MacDiarmid – also known as Christopher Grieve
9. Norman MacCaig in his study

member something in it." He unlocked the door of a bureau
d again, THIRTY-NINE STEPS - I counted them - High tide
ought I had gone mad. "Don't you see it's a clue," I shouted.

1.   2.   3.   4.

1. Burns' manuscript of
   Holy Willie's Prayer
2. Burns, the 'heaven taught
   ploughman'
3. Helen Cruickshank, campaigner
   and poet
4. Robert Louis Stevenson, prolific
   writer and author of novels
   including *Kidnapped* and
   Treasure Island

Both Violet Jacob (1863-1946) and Helen Cruickshank (1886-1975) made major contributions to Scottish poetry and were united in their appreciation of Scottish tradition, using the Scots language to craft their poetry. Jacob's most popular works include *Bonnie Joann* and *Songs of Angus*. Her novels were also well received, with vivid prose and dialogue illuminated by dry wit and humour. Cruickshank was a cultural and political activist as well as a poet, and campaigned passionately for emancipation for women. Her best known poem is *Shy Geordie*, drawing on her own experiences and heritage.

The legacy left by these individuals is continued by contemporary poets such as Don Paterson, Jackie Kay, Robert Crawford, John Burnside and Kathleen Jamie.

Scott, Stevenson and Burns: Scotland's literary heritage

Robert Burns (1759-1796), the 'heaven-taught ploughman', is still hailed as Scotland's national bard more than 200 years after his death, and is celebrated all over the world through translations of his works. Some of his songs, such as *Auld Lang Syne*, are world famous and his *My Love is Like a Red Red Rose* ranks among the finest love-songs ever written. Like Allan Ramsay before him, Burns collected and recorded traditional songs and oral literature. Today Burns is remembered through appreciation societies across the world. His work has become part of international popular culture: *Auld Lang Syne* is the most famous song in the world after *Happy Birthday*. His work has been translated into 50 languages including Arabic, Bashkir, Chinese, Faroese, Icelandic, Uzbek, Japanese and Slovak.

Squire Trelawney, Dr. Livesey, and the rest of these gentlemen having as

from the BEGINNING to the END, keeping nothing back but the BEARIN

6.   7.   8.   9.

Robert Louis Stevenson (1850-1894) savoured the differences between the Old and New Towns, the richer and poorer areas, the urban centre and the rural environs, of his native city. Stevenson was absorbed by Scottish history, geography and character, making them central features of his writing, and although ill health kept him abroad, he continued to write about Scotland. Many of his works examine some of the extreme and contradictory currents of Scotland's history and the subtle psychology he employed in his writing was a precursor for modern literary style. Duality informed much of his work, most famously in *The Strange Case of Dr Jekyll and Mr Hyde*.

A prolific writer, Stevenson was at the height of his career when he died in Samoa, aged 44. His works have been translated into almost every major world language and continue to be adapted for film and television: *Treasure Island*, *The Strange Case of Dr Jekyll and Mr Hyde* and *Kidnapped*.

5. Title page of R.L. Stevenson's *The Strange Case of Dr Jekyll and Mr Hyde*
6. French translation of Robert Louis Stevenson's *Treasure Island*
7. *Kidnapped*, first published in 1886
8. Walter Scott in his study at Castle Street, Edinburgh c.1850
9. Loch Katrine looking towards Ellen's Isle, source of Scott's *The Lady of the Lake*

Overleaf:
The sculpture of Walter Scott at the base of the Scott monument

to write down the whole PARTICULARS about Treasure Island,
the island, and that only because there is still TREASURE not yet lifted

Edinburgh's Walter Scott (1771-1832), recognised in Europe as the creator of the historical novel, was the first British novelist to become a famous public figure. Scott fathered a new type of romantic historiography, and his great influence on Fenimore Cooper (USA), Manzoni (Italy), Balzac and Hugo (France) and the classic Russian novelists is well documented. Scott's appeal lay in his ability to transcend social barriers, as well as those of time and place, to create a gallery and range of characters rivalling those of William Shakespeare and Charles Dickens.

The works that made Scott famous in his own time were the Waverley novels, all set in Scotland from the Union of the Crown of 1707 to the end of the Napoleonic Wars in 1815. The novels, including *Rob Roy* and *Guy Mannering*, are about a people poised between the past and present: they invite readers to reflect on the speed and impact of change. His urge to capture and preserve everything that was strange and wonderful about Scotland both drove his creative ability and his shaping of a modern cultural identity for Scotland. The novels, ballads, poems and other writings of Walter Scott have been translated into almost every major world language. His popularity extended all over the world, even within his own lifetime.

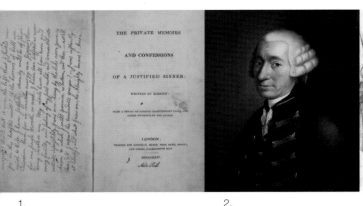

1. 2. 3. 4.

1. Hogg's *Confessions of a Justified Sinner*
2. Tobias Smollett, the first popular Scottish novelist
3. James Hogg, The Ettrick Shepherd, and forerunner of psychological fiction
4. John Home, author of *Douglas*

Breaking the mould: pioneers of fiction

Tobias Smollett (1721-1771) was the first popular Scottish novelist and author of classics *The Adventures of Peregrine Pickle* and *The Expedition of Humphrey Clinker*. His novels were full of grotesque characters, broad satire and witty passages about the low life of Edinburgh. During his lifetime and within 20 years of his death Smollett's works were translated into French, German, Dutch, Polish, Danish, Russian and Italian, and later into Czech, Serbo-Croat, Estonian, Romanian, Slovak, Hungarian, Lithuanian and Bulgarian.

James Hogg (1770-1835) followed Tobias Smollett with a much darker style and is known as the forerunner of psychological fiction. His novel *The Private Memoirs and Confessions of a Justified Sinner* takes the form of the diary of a debased Calvinist who believes himself exempt from all moral law because his eventual admission to heaven is 'justified'. The main character is tempted into increasingly immoral acts by a mysterious stranger – recognisable to the reader as the Devil. During his lifetime, Hogg's works were translated into many languages. This novel ranks with the works of Dostoevsky in its achievement.

The writer and dramatist John Home (1722-1808) is best known for his controversial moral play *Douglas*, which was performed in Edinburgh in 1756 to great acclaim, provoking a member of the audience to cry, 'Whaur's your Wullie Shakespeare noo?' Home was eventually forced by the Church to resign his position as a clergyman because the theatre was still regarded as scandalous.

That STRANGE youth and I approached each other in SILENC eyes. We approached till not more than a yard INTERVENE each other from HEAD to FOOT. What was my astonishme

6.   7.

Born on the Scottish Island of Orkney, Mary Brunton (1778-1818) was the wife of the Edinburgh minister Reverend Alexander Brunton. In Brunton's first novel, *Self Control*, the adventures of her heroines were sugared with a moral message. Her second novel *Discipline* was published in 1814.

Susan Edmonstone Ferrier (1782-1854) was known as the 'Jane Austen of the North'. Her novels challenged the perception that writing by women was frivolous, addressing the role of women in society and the social morals and manners of the age. Her three novels *Marriage, The Inheritance* and *Destiny*, sparkled with intelligence and humour and employed bold satire to great effect. Born in Edinburgh, she was described by Walter Scott as 'simple, full of humour and exceedingly ready at repartee, and all this without the least affectation'.

Margaret Oliphant (1828-1897) continued this mould-breaking tradition as one of the most talented and prolific of the regular contributors to *Blackwood's Magazine*. She was the only female contributor. A shrewd observer of character, her novels addressed the position of women in society. Alongside her numerous articles and stories, her novels placed her in the front rank of Victorian writing.

5. The controversial moral play, *Douglas*
6. Susan Edmonstone Ferrier, the 'Jane Austen of the North', by Augustin Edouart
7. Margaret Oliphant, the only female contributor to *Blackwood's Magazine*

Overleaf:
Zaidee: A Romance by Margaret Oliphant published in *Blackwood's Magazine* (1854-55)

d S L O W L Y , with our eyes FIXED on each other's tween us, and then stood STILL and GAZED, measuring perceiving that he was the SAME being as myself!

The Vivians of the Uplo
well reputed, and of a stately lo
mination some few hundred
had been Castle Vivian a great
trict of the same county, and th
Indistinct adumbrations of
their race had known many a gall
more modest standing ground
much of their original posses
the pretensions of the masters of
grandeur nor impoverished m
pride and glory of being indispu
was a Sir Francis Vivian who
Castle of the race, but Mrs V
out to you the secondary and ob
cousin sprang a .... of th

Family

... were an ancient county family
... ancestral line. At their cul=
... s ago, the family head quarters
... manorial residence in a richer di
... Grange only a jointure house
... were in the family annals, and
... Knights but descended to the
... ral Squires, and denuded of
... age after age had taken from
... Grange. One thing neither redu
... could take from them; the
... heads of the house True it
... held sway in the great old
... ~~the~~ ~~Head~~
... found no difficulty in point
... branch from which this rich

1.   2.   3.

1. One of the earliest surviving manuscripts of *The Brus*, by John Barbour
2. James I and his English wife, an illustration from the Forman Armorial
3. Transcript of *Kingis Quair*, the love poem written by James I

From heroic epics to poignant tragedy: early poetry and the Makars (court poets)

Since the fourteenth century, Scotland's writers have produced literature of international significance. In its earliest form, Scottish literature was dominated by poetry. John Barbour (c.1320-1395) heralded the start of sustained Scots literature and began a national poetic tradition with his epic *The Brus*. This is not only a portrait of Robert Bruce, one of the great figures of the European Middle Ages and a thrilling tale of heroic adventure, but a source of historical information and a textbook on medieval warfare.

King James I of Scotland (c. 1394-1437) was the first Scottish poet to follow the Chaucerian fashion of combining narrative with dream vision. Held for eighteen years in captivity by the English, James I became familiar with the work of Chaucer and married an English noble woman. These events are reflected in his love poem *The Kingis Quair* [The King's Book].

Robert Henryson (c.1425-1508) wrote in a vivid Scots tongue that was particularly suited to conveying tragedy. His most important work was the *Morall Fabillis of Esope the Phyrgian*, a collection of 13 fables.

A! Fredome, The Brus 'A! fredome is a noble thing, Fredo He levys at es that freely levys. A noble hart m failye, for fre liking Is yharnyt our all other thing. Na he t

34 For Dauvit ne'er gaed up til heiven ; he says himsel:
The Lord said tae my lord, Sit ye at my richt haund,

35 Till I mek your faes a fitbrod aneth your feet

36 Let {the haill *(aa)* ~~hoose~~ tawk} o Israel, than, {siccarlie ken} *dout nane.* at God has made him baith Lord an Christ, this same Jesus at ye crucified.

5.

A less serious, but nonetheless technically masterful approach, was taken by William Dunbar (1460-1513). Whether exchanging abuse with other poets in *The Flyting*, sneering at highlanders in *Epetaffe for Donald Owre*, or diverting readers with female conversation in *The Treatis of the Twa Maritt Wemen and the Wedo*, Dunbar has left vivid images of Scotland during the reign of James IV. His *Lament for the Makaris* celebrates many other writers and poets, both English and Scottish.

Gavin Douglas's (c. 1476-1522) most impressive achievement as a poet was his translation of Virgil's *Aeneid* into Scots in 1513. He deploys a hugely imaginative use of Scots to convey the variations of mood and style of the original with outstanding verbal skill. Douglas was the first poet to call his language 'Scottis' as opposed to 'Inglis'. The need to provide a glossary to accompany later editions of *The Eneados* was the stimulus to the lexicography of the Scots language.

The work of critical writers

Many academics associated with the city have done much to raise critical awareness of Scottish literature. Notable amongst these are Sir Herbert Grierson (1866-1960) who advanced the study of Scott, and also the Metaphysical poets. David Daiches (b. 1912) has written widely on Stevenson, Burns and Scott. His autobiographical works recollect his Jewish childhood in Edinburgh.

4. Willam Dunbar's *Book of Poems* printed by Chepman and Myllar
5. Manuscript of *The New Testament* in Scots

ys man to haiff liking, Fredome all solace to man giffis
ff nane es Na ellys nocht that may him ples Gyff fredome
has leyt fre May nocht knaw weill the propyrte'…

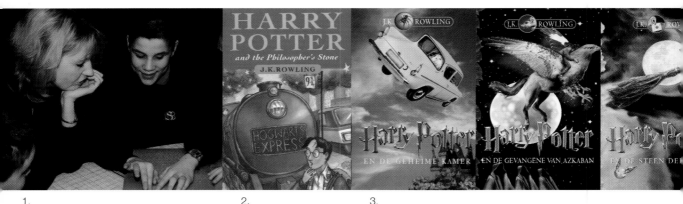

1.   2.   3.

1. A young boy discovers
   Harry Potter through Braille,
   while J.K. Rowling looks on
2. The first book in the
   J.K. Rowling penned series,
   *Harry Potter and the
   Philosopher's Stone*
3. *Harry Potter* titles in Dutch

Wendy and Peter, Ratty and Mole... and the magic of Harry

Edinburgh has long been a centre of children's literature, bringing to life many familiar characters and contributing a number of international classics. Most prominent among these is, of course, *Harry Potter*, the biggest phenomenon in the history of modern publishing. The books have been translated into more than 50 world languages and are sold in 200 countries.

J.K. Rowling wrote the first of the series, *Harry Potter and the Philosopher's Stone*, in a café in Edinburgh. The fifth book of the series, *Harry Potter and the Order of the Phoenix*, was published on 21 June 2003; 1,777,541 copies were sold in the first 24 hours of publication.

However it is not just contemporary writing that inspires children to read. Authors from Edinburgh, or inspired by Edinburgh, have been writing to delight and transport since the 1800s. *Coral Island*, the adventures of three castaways on a South Pacific Island, has been translated into almost every European language and has not been out of print since its original publication in 1858. Its author, Robert Michael Ballantyne (1825-1894), wrote more than 80 adventure stories for boys as well as short stories in magazines and annuals. Born and educated in Edinburgh, Ballantyne lived in the city for most of his life and another famous writer, Robert Louis Stevenson, supported his family when he died.

Peter: What is your name?   *Wendy: (well satisfie*

Peter: Peter Pan. Wendy: Where do you live? *Pet*

5.   6.   7.

If reading is about entering another world, then nothing captures this better than the classic piece of children's literature, J.M. Barrie's *Peter Pan*. A complex work, perceptive and unsentimental about childhood, the book tells us about the 'boy who would not grow up', Wendy, Captain Hook and the Lost Boys of Never Land, all of whom have since been immortalised through countless stage and film versions. The book has been translated into Arabic, Bengali, Chinese, Greek, Japanese, Korean, Russian, Spanish and Turkish.

Another world entirely was given to us by Edinburgh-born Kenneth Grahame (1859-1932), author of *The Wind in the Willows*, renowned for its wonderful characterisation of Toad, Rat, Mole and Badger and their outrageous adventures. The book has not been out of print since it was first published in 1908 and has continued to appeal to successive generations in countries all over the world.

From the willows to the high seas and adventure! Inspired by Edinburgh's Cramond Island, *Treasure Island* is one of the world's most famous children's adventure stories. Reproduced in many film versions, the swashbuckling pirate adventure is a true classic. Robert Louis Stevenson is believed to have used the poet W.E. Henley, a friend and literary collaborator, as the model for the pirate Long John Silver. He also wrote *A Child's Garden of Verses*, inspired by the view over Queen Street Gardens from his childhood home in the New Town of Edinburgh.

4. Peter Pan from J.M. Barrie's
   Peter Pan in Kensington Gardens
   illustrated by Arthur Rackham
5. Ratty and Mole by the fire from
   The Wind in the Willows
6. Portrait of Sir J.M. Barrie
7. Robert Louis Stevenson's
   A Child's Garden of Verses

Overleaf:
The boy who never grew up,
Peter Pan, from the cover of a
1915 edition

Wendy Moira Angela Darling. What's yours?

Second to the right and then straight on till morning.

Chapter 2. The Scottish Enlightenment

Chapter 2

The Scottish Enlightenment

Scotland's outstanding achievement in philosophy, particularly during the period of the Scottish Enlightenment towards the end of the eighteenth century, is one of the great intellectual contributions to world culture. Much of modern philosophy originated in the works of Scottish thinkers of that time, which influenced the whole of the English-speaking world as well as enlightened philosophical movements in Germany and France. Before the eighteenth century was over, Scotland had generated the basic institutions, ideas, attitudes and habits of mind that characterise the modern age, opening a new era in human history.

The very notion of 'human history' itself was largely a Scottish conception. Scots were the first to link history and human nature and present man as a product of history and political environment. In arguing that the study of man is ultimately a scientific one, Scottish philosophers created what are known as the social sciences today: anthropology, ethnography, sociology, psychology, history and economics. Their interest in improving society through an understanding of human nature made an important contribution to contemporary world attitudes towards democracy, freedom and human rights. This age of philosophy is not just an episode in Scottish history: it marks a crucial turning point in the development of the western world.

A hotbed of genius... Edinburgh takes the lead

Edinburgh remained intellectually active throughout the whole period of the enlightenment and attracted talent as the cultural capital of Scotland.

We are conscious that we ourselves, in adapting means to en nor casually we perform these actions, which tend to self pre

2.   3.   4.   5.

Intellectual clubs and societies thrived in Edinburgh, drawing together men with literary and philosophical tastes from all walks of life to exchange ideas and opinions.

Many of Edinburgh's most important intellectual movements began with gatherings in taverns: the Tuesday Club, the Poker Club, the Oyster Club, and the Rankenian Club. The Select Society was the most important Club, welcoming members such as David Hume, Adam Smith, Adam Ferguson and Lord Kames. For ten years it was the central forum of Edinburgh's 'republic of letters'.

Famously called a 'hotbed of genius', Edinburgh's close-knit community of scholars and thinkers was unique and attracted outsiders such as Adam Smith, Benjamin Franklin and Robert Burns. Only London and Paris could compete with Edinburgh as an intellectual centre, but Edinburgh stood out as a city where intellect rather than social rank mattered: a place where a farmer like Robert Burns could be embraced as a member of the literati.

The literature produced by Scots, and especially Edinburgh writers, exceeded in quality and quantity what could have been expected from such a small country. The works of the Scots were reviewed in the major European philosophical journals as soon as they appeared and were soon translated into other languages. In this way Scottish thought was quickly given a wide audience in Europe, and was assimilated by German philosophers in particular.

1. Robert Burns, associated with Enlightenment figures
2. David Hume, one of the key members of the Select Society
3. Lord Kames, leading Enlightenment figure
4. Adam Ferguson, also a member of the Select Society
5. Adam Smith, another famous participant of the Select Society meetings

guided by REASON and DESIGN, that 'tis not ignorantly
ion to the obtaining of PLEASURE, and avoiding PAIN.

1. 2. 3.

1. German translation of *A Treatise of Human Nature*, David Hume
2. David Hume's *A Treatise of Human Nature*, in English
3. Salisbury Crags, inspiration for James Hutton's theories

The thirst for understanding

The first steps in world-changing thought were taken by Adam Smith (1723 - 1790) in his pioneering economics work. Yet it was his *Theory of Moral Sentiments* that made him truly famous – held to be as important as Freud's *Interpretation of Dreams* in the field of psychology.

David Hume (1711-1776) is remembered as modernity's first great philosopher. For more than 2,000 years Western philosophers had praised the primacy of reason as the guide to all human emotion and virtue. Hume reversed this with his book *A Treatise of Human Nature*, writing that 'reason is, and ought to be, the slave of the passions'. Hume tried to banish religion from the discussion of moral and social conduct. However, this provoked a large opposition – the Scottish Common Sense movement, led by Thomas Reid. He was a moderate clergyman from Aberdeen who refuted that common sense overcame reason. Reid's impact in America was huge; Thomas Jefferson borrowed Reid's idea of 'self-evident truths' for the US Declaration of Independence.

Jefferson was also influenced by Francis Hutcheson (1694-1746), who saw the ultimate goal of liberty as happiness, prompting him to add 'the pursuit of happiness' to his list of the inalienable rights of man. Hutcheson's writings challenged all forms of oppression and inspired anti-slavery abolitionists throughout the UK and USA. Together with the work of Hutcheson, it was those of Henry Home, Lord Kames (1696-1782) that revolutionised the Scots intellect.

...that every creature which God has made, in the **heavens** earth is an individual! What **exists** is an **individual.** Univers

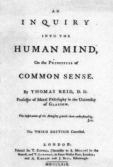

5.   6.   7.   8.

Kames organised the history of human community into four distinct stages and showed how each environment forces changes in the way people think, act and govern their lives. William Robertson (1721-1793) later used Kames' four-stage theory in creating the study of modern history.

Moving people... moving the earth

Reid's greatest pupil, Dugald Stewart (1753-1828) developed Reid's Common Sense Philosophy; in merging Adam Smith's moral realism with Reid's common sense, he creating the principles of political science. Through Dugald Stewart, Scottish philosophy touched almost every aspect of public life in Britain, as well as extending across the English-speaking world and colonies. By the 1790s its principles were being taught in every Scottish university, were gaining favour in America and France and profoundly influenced the intellectual environment of Immanuel Kant in Germany.

The roots of another school of thought altogether were also borne out of Scotland. Adam Ferguson (1723-1816) studied in Edinburgh for the clergy. His *Essay on the History of Civil Society* contained one of the first uses of the word 'civilisation' in English, coining the term 'civil society' as synonymous with modernity. Marxism owes its greatest debt to Ferguson as the most trenchant critic of capitalism.

Whereas Stewart and Ferguson looked at the progress of man, James Hutton (1726-1797) looked at the progress of the earth. His study of the rocks and mountains around Edinburgh led him to a new understanding of the science of geology.

4. Portrait of Dugald Stewart, Thomas Reid's greatest pupil
5. Swedish translation of Adam Ferguson's *Essay on the History of Civil Society*
6. Thomas Reid's *Inquiry into the Human Mind*
7. Swedish translation of William Robertson's *History of America*
8. William Robertson, historian

ove, or in the earth beneath, or in the waters under the
e not individuals and, therefore, universals do not exist.

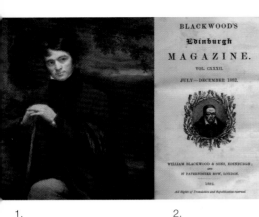   

1.   2.   3.   4.   5.

1. Thomas Carlyle, by John Linnell
2. Title page from *Blackwood's Magazine* 1882 edition
3. John Wilson, who wrote under the literary disguise of 'Christopher North'
4. Robert Burns, whose *A Man's a Man for A' That* encapsulated enlightened notions
5. Henry Mackenzie, whose *The Man of Feeling* was a book Burns 'prized next to the Bible'

His *Theory of the Earth* concluded that the Earth's crust was made up of the debris of past geological upheavals and was much older than the Bible suggested. He set the stage for the study of evolution, embraced by his contemporary Erasmus Darwin, and later by his grandson, Charles Darwin – also an Edinburgh student – in his seminal work *On the Origin of Species*.

Enlightened writing and literature

Against this background of development and continuing enlightenment, Edinburgh's literary community was inspired to comment and contribute through writing. *Blackwood's Magazine* was home to John Wilson (1785-1854), who under the literary disguise of 'Christopher North' wrote fearsome and witty reviews and commentaries on prominent figures of the day. After his death in 1854, literary Scotland was a notably quieter place.

Another critic, historian and essayist of the Enlightenment was Thomas Carlyle (1795-1881), whose writings offer a valuable insight into this period. One of his most influential pieces was *Heroes and Hero Worship* in which he identified the need for heroes to lead a society that had lost its way. Carlyle's effect on writers of his time was extraordinary: many Victorian novels bear the imprint of his analysis, including the works of Dickens, Thackeray, Eliot and Disraeli in the UK and European writers, Proust, Baudelaire and Fröding. In seeking to express the new philosophy of the Enlightenment, great literature emerged.

I think that the Time we spent there, was Six Weeks of the dens
and instructive Society we found there in such Plenty, has left
Connections draw me elsewhere, I believe Scotland would be t

7.   8.

Much of the poetry of Robert Burns encapsulated enlightened notions of the time: for instance the democratic principles of *A Man's A Man for A' That*. Burns himself commented that Henry Mackenzie's *The Man of Feeling* was 'a book I prize next to the bible'. The carefully defined sentimentalism encouraged by the Enlightenment was reflected throughout the novel in the sensitivity of the hero, Harley.

The Scots' thirst for understanding produced the *Encyclopaedia Britannica* in Edinburgh in 1768. The world's leading reference source still displays its thistle emblem today.

Enlightened times... enlightened visitors

Among the many international visitors to Edinburgh during the Enlightenment was Benjamin Franklin, who was honoured with the freedom of the city during his first visit in 1759. Many American visitors followed Franklin, and around 100 students came to the University of Edinburgh in the years leading up to the American Revolution.

A later visitor was the American ornithologist John James Audubon, who came to Britain in 1826 seeking an engraver capable of reproducing the paintings for his book *The Birds of America*. It was in Edinburgh that he found the necessary encouragement and facilities to realise his ambitions, meeting William Home Lizars, the engraver who demonstrated the feasibility of printing and publishing the large paintings, and William MacGillivray, conservator at the museum of the Royal College of Surgeons of Edinburgh, who assisted Audubon in writing the Ornithological Bibliography.

6. The famous thistle emblem of the *Encyclopaedia Britannica*
7. *The Man of Feeling*, by Henry Mackenzie
8. Detail from an illustration from *The Birds of America*, by John James Audubon, who sought expertise in Edinburgh for his book

Overleaf:
David Hume writes at his desk.
Engraving by Louis Carrogis

ppiness I have met with in any Part of my Life. And the agreeable asing an Impression on my Memory, that did not strong untry I should chuse to spend the Remainder of my Days in.

Chapter 3. Edinburgh as a centre of publishing

Chapter 3

Edinburgh as a centre of publishing

The diffusion of ideas during the Scottish Enlightenment and the international impact of Scots thinkers would not have been possible without Edinburgh's pioneering publishers. As an historic centre of innovative publishing, printing and bookselling, Edinburgh gave writers access to a localised print network that could produce and distribute their work on a wide scale.

After the stranglehold of London publishers over copyright privileges in Britain was lifted in 1774, there was a surge of Scottish publishing activity that built on the success of early pioneers. Since then, the book trade has always played an important part in the local economy. In 1763 there were six publishing houses in Edinburgh for a population of 60,000. By 1790 there were 16 publishing houses and today there are over 80 publishing companies in Edinburgh, whose population has grown to 450,000.

The very first printing press was set up by Androw Myllar and Walter Chepman in 1507, and printing continued to gather momentum throughout the fifteen hundreds. By the seventeenth century, Scottish printing grew further, spreading to Glasgow and Aberdeen, although Edinburgh retained its pre-eminence. The eighteenth century was a period of creativity and elegance and Edinburgh became a world centre of excellence for book-binding. William Creech, an extraordinarily successful businessman, published the works of major figures of the Enlightenment at this time, as well as giving national and international circulation to the poems of Burns.

The activity has grown from small beginnings into dissemination of all manner of cultural material;

2.   3.   4.   5.

For a time, Edinburgh challenged London as the main centre of publishing in Britain. A belief in the printed word as an instrument of education and progress in society and the presence of ambitious early publishers helped create the boom.

The business of writing

Archibald Constable (1774-1827) began as a bookseller's apprentice in Edinburgh and published both the *Edinburgh Review* and the *Encyclopaedia Britannica*. But it was his business acumen combined with the creative energy of Walter Scott that created his most successful partnership. 6,000 copies of *Waverley* were sold in the first six months, and 2,000 of *Guy Mannering* within a day of publication.

Like Constable, William Blackwood (1776-1834) started as a bookseller's apprentice. He is best remembered as the founder of *Blackwood's Magazine*, which predated Victorian periodicals in publishing contemporary fiction serially.

Many of today's global publishing houses have their origins in Edinburgh, including Chambers, Nelson, John Murray and A. & C. Black. Yet another bookseller's assistant who began with barely a penny to his name started the first of these. William Chambers (1800-1883) partnered his brother Robert, a talented and prolific writer, most famously publishing *Chambers Encyclopaedia*. The Nelson mentioned is Thomas Nelson, who employed one of the first travelling representatives in Scottish publishing. His son continued the tradition of innovation by using the railway network to sell books throughout Britain.

1. Thomas Nelson and Sons' colophon
2. William Creech, publisher, who gave national and international circulation to the poems of Burns
3. The printer's device of Androw Myllar, who set up the first printing press with Walter Chepman in 1507
4. Archibald Constable, painted by Andrew Geddes
5. *Waverley*, which sold 6,000 copies in its first six months of publication

AST and complex industry responsible for the pact upon civilization is impossible to calculate.

1.

2.

3.

4.

1. Francis Jeffrey, in whose home *The Edinburgh Review* was established in 1802
2. John Murray I, founder of one of the UK's leading publishing houses
3. David Livingstone, missionary and explorer, whose work features in the extensive John Murray archives
4. David Livingstone is rescued from his brush with the lion

Established in 1768, John Murray Ltd was one of the leading British publishing houses with an unrivalled list of authors. The National Library of Scotland has submitted a leading bid to acquire the John Murray Archive, a national treasure consisting of over 150,000 items, papers and manuscripts of writers published since the company was founded.

The writers include some of the greatest world figures from the past 200 years, including Jane Austen, Charles Darwin, David Livingstone and Lord Byron. The Scottish Executive has pledged £6.5 million towards the bid, and a decision about an application to the National Lottery Fund is expected in early 2005.

Finally, Adam Black (1784-1874) purchased both the *Encyclopaedia Britannica* and the copyright and stock of Walter Scott's works to enable his business to expand and diversify. From its London base it continues to specialise in reference publications.

Collins and Macmillan and Co. were founded in Glasgow. William Collins was sold to Rupert Murdoch for $717 million in 1988: a far cry from the days of those penniless apprentices!

Scandal, gossip and criticism – all in the name of art

The Edinburgh Review was established in 1802 at Francis Jeffrey's house in Buccleuch Place, Edinburgh. Published first in Edinburgh but later in London it appeared quarterly, setting a new standard in criticism.

A ghost is a sign of importance not
as much as a small farm to the comp

6.   7.   8.

At its height it reached a circulation of 14,000; some issues were so popular that they were reprinted up to ten times. *The Edinburgh Review* was the most influential literary journals of its time in the English-speaking world. Walter Scott and Thomas Carlyle were contributors to the *Review*, which was circulated all over the British Empire. International readers included Thomas Jefferson, James Madison and Samuel Adams in America.

Blackwood's Magazine, established in 1817 as a conservative response to the liberal politics of *The Edinburgh Review*, was a permanent feature of literary life in Edinburgh for 150 years. Founded by William Blackwood, the magazine owed much of its success to its talented young editors, John Gibson Lockhart and John Wilson whose sharp satire and parody turned the magazine into the most shocking and best-selling review of its time. *Blackwood's Magazine* went on to attract internationally acclaimed writers including Thomas De Quincey (who spent the last 30 years of his life in Edinburgh), Joseph Conrad, Anthony Trollope, Henry James, Oscar Wilde, John Buchan, JB Priestley, Neville Shute, and serialised all but one of George Eliot's novels.

Chambers' Edinburgh Journal, begun in 1832, was the first cheap periodical of an educational nature widely accessed by the masses. Its phenomenal success belied the Scottish taste for learning. Published by William and Robert Chambers, the journal was one of the most popular of the Victorian age, with a circulation of 50,000 – 80,000 copies. It pioneered a new form of serious but inexpensive periodical publishing.

5. Thomas De Quincey, one of the internationally acclaimed writers who lived in Edinburgh for the last 30 years of his life

6. Oscar Wilde, sometime contributor to *Blackwood's Magazine*

7. Thomas Carlyle, another famous contributor to *Blackwood's Magazine*

8. John Gibson Lockhart, one of the talented young editors of *Blackwood's Magazine* and son-in-law of Sir Walter Scott

e despised; a haunted room is worth

ncy of the family that owns it.

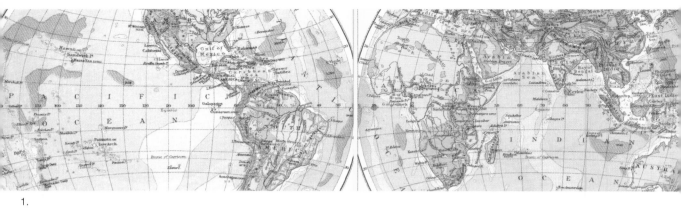

1.

1. The worldwide influence of the Scots – felt in every corner of the globe

Spreading the word

The Scots, with their strong commitment to education and the printed word, and a long tradition of publishing, carried these ideals with them to all corners of the world during the eighteenth century. As immigrants to America, Canada, Australia and colonial visitors in India and Africa, Scots established newspapers, and recorded important literature celebrating local culture and languages for posterity.

In America it was a Scot, John Campbell, who published the first regular newspaper in America, the Boston Newsletter. Almost 200 years later in 1801, another Scotsman, Alexander Hamilton began the *New York Post* – which is still being published today. James Gordon Bennett – no doubt as to his place of birth – sometimes called the father of modern American journalism, was the first to print a financial article, had the first society page and was the first to employ European correspondents for his *New York Herald*, the predecessor of the *Herald Tribune*.

Many newspapers proliferated in British India, some of which remain classics of the world press. The *Bombay Gazette* was founded by John Stevenson, the first person sent to India by the Scottish Missionary Society, and edited by another Scotsman, Dr George Buist. Scots also played an important part in the printing and grammar of Indian language. John Borthwick Gilchrist, born in Edinburgh, instructed in Urdu and Hindistani. By deciding to use Devanagari script for his *Hindustani Dictionary*, Gilchrist established the alphabet currently used for printing Hindi.

I saw a triangle slicing the water fifteen feet away. It wa
and down my spine. I swam as fast as I could to one enc
myself up on the lifebuoy with my arms. I couldn't s

3.   4.   5.   6.

A second flowering

The last 30 years has seen a resurgence in growth of Scottish publishing. Around 90 companies and organisations publish books in Scotland, with the trade remaining firmly rooted in Edinburgh. The greatest focus of Scottish publishing is on reference, academic and scientific books – a sector in which Scottish publishers have excelled since the days when *Encyclopaedia Britannica* was started. However, a third of Scottish publishers publish fiction, producing disproportionate numbers of international bestsellers.

As the home of a vibrant publishing industry, Edinburgh plays host to 50 publishing houses. Contemporary companies such as Canongate Books, Mainstream and Birlinn with its Polygon imprint have maintained Edinburgh's international publishing profile with strong new imprints selling rights internationally. Polygon has published many internationally acclaimed books, including the best-selling *The No. 1 Ladies' Detective Agency* by Alexander McCall Smith. Canongate Books is one of Edinburgh's – and Scotland's – biggest business success stories. The company came to prominence in 2002 when it became the first Scottish publisher to win the Booker Prize with *Life of Pi*. On the back of this, it was also awarded Publisher of the Year at the British Book Awards in 2003.

Scottish publishers have continued to innovate. Together with new media specialists, Screenbase, Canongate have pioneered animated book promotions on the Internet and in film, bringing new titles to a wider audience. This initiative has attracted worldwide attention and is tipped to spearhead a global trend.

2. *Chambers Pocket Dictionary*, one of the many reference books published in Scotland

3. McCall Smith's *The Full Cupboard of Life*, published by Polygon

4. *A Highland Lady in France*, re-published by the leading Scottish history publisher, Tuckwell Press, first published in 1898

5. Re-print of Neil M. Gunn's *Sun Circle* first published in 1933

6. Scottish publishers produce a wide range of titles, from academic to fiction

Overleaf:
Cover detail from Booker Prize winning novel *Life of Pi*, published by Canongate Books. Painting by Andy Bridge.

ark's fin. An awful tingle, cold and liquid, went up

e lifeboat, the end still covered by the tarpaulin. I pushed

chard Parker. He wasn't on the tarpaulin or on a bench.

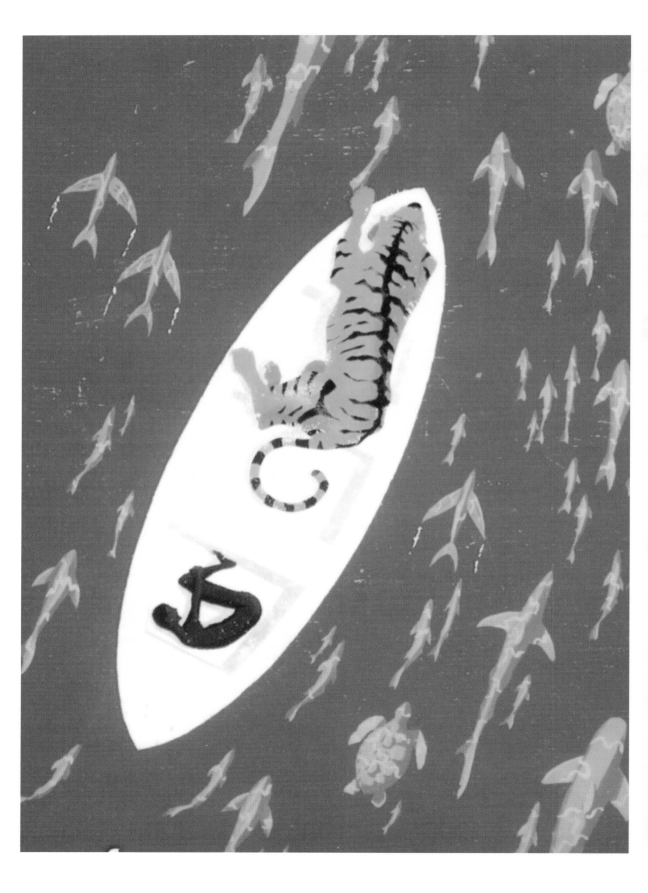

Chapter 4. Scotland: A literate nation with a love of books

Chapter 4
Scotland: A literate nation with a love of books

Scotland was one of the first literate societies in Europe. Educational pioneers in Scotland recognised literacy as a basic right and used it as a tool to lift men, women and children in Scotland from poverty and to achieve equality of opportunity.

In 1496 the Scottish Parliament passed the world's first compulsory education law, obliging each freeholder to send his eldest son to school at six years old. But literacy and education remained the preserve of the aristocracy and the Church.

In the sixteenth century the concept of compulsory education was carried further with the egalitarian principles of the religious reformer John Knox, who proposed that education be accessible, comprehensive, democratic and free to all of ability. By the early 1700s reading was offering access to ideas and experiences which would broaden the mental horizons of most Scots and enable them to engage with issues far beyond their community. As the century advanced, a further dimension to literacy emerged in the shape of imaginative literature, offering stimulus and pleasure as the motivation for reading, and also writing.

By the 1790s, almost all Scots could read, regardless of wealth, gender, status or location. Visitors to Scotland were surprised at the widespread literacy and reading tastes of the Scottish public.

What though on hamely fare we dine, Wear hoddin grey, an' a' th for a' that. For a' that, an' a' that, Their tinsel show, an' a' th

2. 3. 4.

It was observed that even servant girls had copies of Burns' poems and other popular literature of the day, and people of the most modest means had their own collection of books. What they could not buy, they borrowed from libraries – each sizeable town had one, following the precedent set by Allan Ramsay in Edinburgh. Dr Samuel Johnson noted in a visit to the remote Hebridean Islands that he 'never encountered a house in which he did not find books in more languages than one'.

Literacy opened up new cultural choices. Records from the library at Innerpeffray in Perthshire between 1747 and 1800 show books loaned to the local baker, the blacksmith, the cooper, the dyer and his apprentice, to farmers, stonemasons, tailors and household servants. The books borrowed were a balance between the religious and the secular.

In the 1860s, 1 in 140 of the Scottish population received a secondary education and 1 in 1,000 attended University. Scotland's dedication to advanced education is long-standing and its universities are among the oldest in the world. From 1720 to 1840 the student population of Scotland trebled.

1. Statue of John Knox in the quadrangle of New College, Edinburgh
2. Image from Dr Thomas Guthrie's Ragged School in Edinburgh
3. Allan Ramsay, owner of the first lending library
4. Dr Samuel Johnson and James Boswell depicted in Edinburgh's High Street en route to the Hebrides

ie fools their silks, and knaves their wine,   A man's a man

ne honest man, tho' e'er sae poor,   Is king o' men for a' that.

1.   2.   3.

1. Craighouse at Napier University,
   Edinburgh
2. New buildings on the
   Heriot-Watt University
   Campus, Edinburgh
3. Matthew Taylor from Peterhead
   is introduced to the largest book
   in his local library

As university education was relatively cheap, many students came from working backgrounds. Lectures were open to the public, and attending classes became a hobby among the townspeople: education was intended to be truly egalitarian.

The story of education in the twentieth century throughout the UK became the search to extend to all children, and later to all adults, equality of opportunity. Literacy was the cornerstone of that education. In the late twentieth century, the definition of literacy in Scotland expanded to include talking and listening skills and the study of the media, as well as a recognition of the importance of the culture and language of the local community. A unique assessment was designed for schools to achieve equality of opportunity for all children, mirrored by a determination to increase opportunities for late learners in the adult population, and to make Higher Education possible for an increasing number of people.

Today Edinburgh retains its status as a seat of education and is home to three Universities – the University of Edinburgh, Napier University and Heriot-Watt University, all of which are internationally renowned research and teaching centres.

Harry didn't even care that Draco Malfoy was maki
Slytherin table. With a bit of luck. Malfoy woul

5.

6.

Inspiring a love of reading

Data from a 1996 literacy survey concluded that roughly half of the Scottish population reads books each week. To ensure that this statistic continues to grow, Scottish literature organisations work in partnership with educational programmes and local authorities to promote readership from the earliest ages.

Bookstart is the first national books-for-babies programme in the world. It provides books for every new baby born in the UK and offers advice to parents on sharing books with their children.

J.K. Rowling, a Reading Champion for the Scottish Executive's Home Reading initiative, which encourages parents and carers to share books with children, sums up why this work is so important.

'It's the simplest and most magical thing to turn a page and be transported to a whole new world; see things through someone else's eyes; and learn something you couldn't find out any other way'.

UNESCO's World Book Day was marked in over 30 countries around the globe last year. In the UK, a main aim of the day, celebrated in March, is to encourage children to explore the pleasures of reading by providing them with the opportunity to have a book of their own.

National Poetry Day, celebrated in October, is marked in Scotland by the distribution of half a million free poetry postcards.

4. Storyteller Amu at one of Scotland's many literature festivals

5/6. Deep in books at the Edinburgh International Book Festival

...d, snide remarks about his new jumper from the

...etting his come-uppance in a few hours' time.

1. 2. 3. 4.

1. Children at an Edinburgh International Book Festival sale
2/4. From a series of postcards produced by the Scottish Poetry Library
3. Reading on the lawn at the Edinburgh International Book Festival

Other initiatives aimed at children include the annual Summer Reading Challenge in libraries, in which children are encouraged to read at least six books during the holidays for a medal, and various resources on the web.

The activities of organisations like Scottish Book Trust, Scottish Storytelling Centre and Scottish Poetry Library range from a touring poetry van to writers' and storytellers' events throughout Scotland. The current Children's Laureate, Michael Morpurgo, visited city centre and remote island schools and libraries all over Scotland in 2004, giving over 6,000 children, teachers and librarians the chance to meet one of the UK's most popular authors.

For those who had a limited initial education, or who missed out on learning to read through other disadvantages, there are a number of projects aimed at enhancing their reading and writing skills. These include CLAN, aimed especially at young adults, those facing redundancy and people with health problems affecting their ability to engage in reading, 'Branching Out', a project to support reader development professionals in delivering their services and 'A Touch Of...', which aims to increase access to literature for the blind.

The enthusiasm of Edinburgh people for literature is demonstrated by the wealth of book, poetry and writing groups in the city. Book groups are mostly private gatherings between friends, but agencies like the City of Edinburgh Library Service organise some of the city's largest reading groups. The Shore Poets meet monthly in an historic Edinburgh tavern to hear readings.

Some smooth Some rough Som
stones with colours glowing Like diam

6.   7.

Living through literature

Scotland has a burgeoning number of literary events and festivals that fuel enthusiasm for the written word – according to research, 80,000 people attend two or more literary events in Scotland every year.

The Edinburgh International Book Festival forms the central part of a year-round calendar of literary events across Scotland. Throughout its 21-year history, the Book Festival has grown rapidly in size and scope to become the largest and most dynamic festival of its kind in the world. One of the festival's hallmarks is the series of high profile debates and discussions. Each year writers from all over the world gather to become part of this unique forum in which audience and author meet to exchange thoughts and opinions. Hundreds of leading international writers have been presented at the Book Festival, including Gore Vidal, Alan Bennett, Louis de Bernieres, Seamus Heaney, Doris Lessing, Muriel Spark and Harold Pinter. The Children's Fair is an integral part of the event, and showcases writers and illustrators for young people.

Scotland is well served by literature festivals. An annual poetry festival, StAnza, is held in St Andrews; Cromarty Book Festival in the Highlands; the WORD festival in Aberdeen; Wigtown Book Town Festival celebrates its status as Scotland's National Book Town every September; and the Scottish International Storytelling Festival back in Edinburgh celebrates storytelling traditions from around the world.

5. Storywriting at the Edinburgh International Book Festival
6. Poem postcard
7. Sculpture at Leaderfoot by Garry Tay, poem by Valerie Gillies

Overleaf:
A poster for the third Edinburgh Book Festival, illustrated by Michael Foreman

arkly Cool but friendly Ancient
ds. Makes me feel Joined to the past.

Chapter 5. Scotland's unique languages

Chapter 5
Scotland's unique languages

A unique voice for Scotland

The Scots and Gaelic languages are unique to Scotland. The Scots tongue has been the vehicle for some of Scotland's outstanding literary works, and its wealth of colourful vocabulary and idiom have conveyed the fiery imagination, intellect, stoicism and affection of the Scottish character to the world. During the Middle Ages, Scots was the official language of the courts, of state, and of kings. Following the Union in 1707, English became the language of government and polite society. This trend continued into the Enlightenment, when the use of English implied elevated class status. However, the continued use of Scots in popular poetry and fiction had a major impact on the Scottish people's sense of identity and kept their culture intact. It is the living language spoken daily by millions of Scots.

Although Gaelic is now spoken by only a small fraction of the Scottish population, it has a cultural profile and influence far greater than such a statistic might suggest. Gaelic has contributed a wealth of cultural assets to the nation in terms of music, songs, dance, poetry and storytelling. Although Scots is a language used nowhere else in the world and recognised by the European Bureau for Lesser-Used Languages, Gaelic endures today in Nova Scotia.

Scotland faces similar cultural issues to many countries with endangered languages. Like other cultures seeking to preserve their linguistic heritage in the face of mass communication, Scotland needs to build public awareness and appreciation for its minority languages.

Aunt Julia spoke Gaelic   very LOUD and very *FAST*.   By
BLACK   of a sandy GRAVE at Luskentyre.   But I hear her s
yards   of peatscapes and lazybeds   and getting ANGRY, gett

As a World City of Literature, Edinburgh would seek to enhance awareness of Scots and Gaelic languages both at home and abroad and share their distinctive and colourful nature with a global audience.

1. Gaelic writing taken from *The Great Book of Gaelic*, (An Leabhar Mòr) published by Canongate Books

Not just for flichtmafletheries

The Scots language ('the mither tongue') is descended from Old Northumbrian, the northern form of Old English. It has been influenced by Norse, Gaelic and Dutch. In Scots an agile turn of phrase, the sound of the words and their choice are thought to be almost as important as their meanings.

The Scots language exploits the emotive power of the sounds of words to an extent that has no parallel in Western European languages. Words like flichtmafletheries (useless or excessive ornamentation), heeligoleerie (in a confused state) and cattiewurrie (a noisy dispute) give a real sense of their meaning. Scots is a language of verbal creativity that speaks in vivid tones, particularly suited to the linguistic inventiveness of Scots poetry.

The wider variety of sound patterns allowed by the Scots language meant it was exploited with great skill by the court poets of the Middle Ages, the Makars, such as John Barbour, Robert Henryson and William Dunbar.

e I had learned   a little, she lay   silenced in the absolute

lcoming me   with a seagull's VOICE   across a hundred

NGRY   with so many questions UNANSWERED.

Allan Ramsay and others in the early eighteenth century drew attention to the glories of early poetry in the Scots language. And its stature has been further increased by poets such as Robert Fergusson, Robert Burns and Hugh MacDiarmid (aka Christopher Grieve) and by novelists such as Sir Walter Scott, James Hogg, John Galt, Robert Louis Stevenson and Lewis Grassic Gibbon. The strength of literary Scots has never been greater than it is today, with authors such as William McIlvanney, Liz Lochhead and Irvine Welsh drawing freely on the language in their writing.

Music for the Blind Harper

Gaelic has been spoken in Scotland for over 1,500 years, having been brought over by Celtic migrants. The language spread and developed into a distinct Scottish version. Scottish Gaelic is strongly idiomatic and also possesses a great variety of sounds. Gaelic word order is also slightly different from that of many other European languages, with the verb often appearing at the start of a sentence.

The earliest surviving evidence of a distinct Scottish Gaelic tradition appears in an anthology of heroic sagas, ballads and ecclesiastical texts, *The Book of the Dean of Lismore*, compiled in the early fifteen hundreds by Sir James MacGregor. In the seventeenth century Scottish Gaelic poetry flowered with many poets including An Clarsair Dall (the Blind Harper).

Is scich mo chrob ón scríbainn; ní digainn mo glés geroll;
Sceithid penn = gulban caelda = di ndaelda do dub glégorm.

Bruinnid srúaim n-ecna ndedairn as mo láim degduin desmais;
Dointíd a dig for duilinn do dub in chuilinn chnesglais.

Sinim mo phenn   mbec mbraenach tar aenoch lebar ligoll
Cen scor fri selba   ségonn, diann scíth mo chrob ón scríbonn.

My hand tires of writing, this pen is not steady,
though its narrow beak spouts a dark stream of blue ink.

This brown skilful hand pours out endless wisdom
in holly-tree ink flowing over each page.

Driving wet wee pen through market of fine books,
not stopping for pay from the rich, my hand tires of writing.

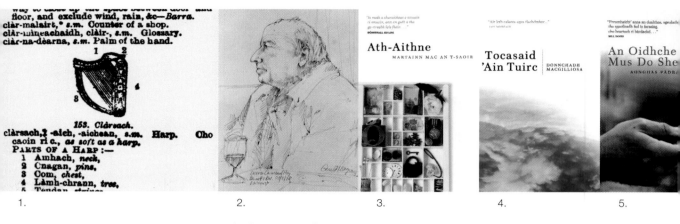

1.

2.

3.

4.

5.

1. An entry from the illustrated Gaelic-English Dictionary by Edward Dwelly
2. George Campbell Hay, one of the notable contemporary writers of the twentieth century
3. *Ath-Aithne*, Saltire Award Winner 2003 and part of the New Gaelic Fiction series
4. *Tocasaid 'Ain Tuire*, part of the New Gaelic Fiction series
5. *An Oidhche Mus Do Sheòl Sinn*, part of the New Gaelic Fiction series

Interest in Gaelic culture has never really died, but contact with other literature in the eighteenth century brought new vigour to Scottish Gaelic writing. Probably the most significant Gaelic poet of the century was Alexander Macdonald, whose *Ais-eiridh na Sean Chanoin Albannaich* (The Resurrection of the Ancient Scottish Tongue) was the first book of secular poetry printed in Scotland.

Notable contemporary Gaelic writing began to appear in periodicals in the late nineteenth century, followed in the twentieth century by the publication of writers like Iain Crichton Smith, Sorley MacLean, Angus Nicholson, George Campbell Hay and Derick Thomson. Gaelic writers included Donald MacAulay, Aonghas MacNeacail, Meg Bateman, Rody Gorman and Kevin MacNeil.

Ensuring even small voices are heard

Gaelic is technically an endangered language: there are fewer than 60,000 Gaelic speakers in Scotland and this number is decreasing. However, the Scottish Executive has appointed a Minister with special responsibility for Gaelic and works closely with Gaelic bodies like the Bord Na Gaidhlig (Gaelic Council) to promote the language and assist in its development. Gaelic now features at all levels of education in Scotland and as part of teacher training.

O Allt na Fearnaibh gus an fhaoilinn Tha soilleir an dìomnaireachd nam bea

A'tilleadh a Hallaig anns an fheasgar Anns a chamhanaich bhalbh bh

33 Thae tarmegantis, with tag and atter,
Full loud in Ersche began to clatter,
And rowp lyk revin and ruke.
The devil sa devit was with thair yell,
That in the depest pot of hell
He smorit thame with smuke.

William Dunbar (c.1460–c.1520), The
Daunce of the Sevin Deidly Sinnis

7.   8.   9.

The language itself is no longer confined to small pockets in rural areas but is established in main urban areas. There are around 150 hours of Gaelic language programming a year on Scottish television and public documents and road signs in the north of Scotland are often reproduced in Gaelic.

Gaelic publishing has a long history (the first book was printed in 1567) and more books than ever before are being produced. *Gath* magazine, containing short stories and other material from popular Gaelic writers, is published in Edinburgh and is gaining in popularity.

Scots, however, is a language of everyday life, with 30% of Scottish people believed to use it. Recently this rich and expressive tongue has seen renewed interest from Parliament, education, media and society. Scots-language titles are to be found in around a third of publishers in Scotland. One of the most inventive publishers for children is Itchy Coo Books, an imprint of Black & White Publishing, which publishes 'braw books for bairns o aw ages'.

6. *Gath* Magazine,
   published in Edinburgh for a
   growing Gaelic readership
7. *King o' the Midden*, one of the
   innovative Scots titles from
   Itchy Coo Books.
8. Title page from *A Scots Dialect
   Dictionary*
9. Scots, a language of creativity –
   An extract from the *Pocket
   Book of Scottish Quotations*
   by David Ross

Overleaf:
Hugh MacDiarmid sculpture at
Langholm in the Scottish Borders

han eil ab coimhthional nan nighean   Ag cumail na coiseadhd gun dheann.
'lìonadh nan leathadan casa,   An gàireachdaich 'nam chluais 'na ceò,

Chapter 6. A city of remembrance and inspiration

Chapter 6
A city of remembrance and inspiration

The literary life of Edinburgh remains vibrant, with contemporary publishers and literature organisations thriving alongside historical institutions. The city's history is steeped in literary associations, and several of the streets and their inhabitants have inspired and featured in classic works of literature.

In one square mile in the historic centre of the city – the Old Town – is an area that for more than 500 years has formed the nucleus of Scotland's literary activity. From Holyrood Palace, the site of Scotland's first printing press, to the Mercat Cross, home of the first lending library, through the myriad of closes in Canongate and around the Royal Mile that housed literary societies, libraries and publishing houses, the history of literature seems very much alive.

In the same fertile ground where the Scottish Enlightenment was cultivated 250 years earlier, a new 'Literature Quarter' is growing. Organisations such as the National Library of Scotland, the Scottish Poetry Library, Scottish Storytelling Centre, Scottish Book Trust, Edinburgh University Library, Central Library, Canongate Books, the Saltire Society, the Writers' Museum and Makar's Court, make up the heart of Edinburgh's city of literature.

Opposite
Greyfriars Bobby, who inspired the novel of the same name by Eleanor Atkinson

1.

2.

There are many symbols of Edinburgh's rich literary history visible in the city today, from plaques and statues to streets that still bear the names of those honoured for their literary achievements. In punctuating the city with their presence these testaments to literature-past colour our present environment.

Edinburgh's monument to Walter Scott is, at 60 metres high, the largest in the world to a literary figure. Edinburgh is unique in naming its main rail terminal, Waverley Station, after a novel. And another famous literary son is honoured with a monument atop Calton Hill – the Burns Memorial, and a stained glass window in St Giles Cathedral, dedicated to the 'poet of humanity'. The magnificent Greek Temple that shares Calton Hill was built in honour of Dugald Stewart, an important contributor to the Enlightenment.

Walk through Princes Street Gardens, and you'll be joined by a host of literary figures. A serene grove of trees enclosed by a stone wall pays tribute to Robert Louis Stevenson; a statue to Allan Ramsay stands in the Gardens before his distinctive 'Goose Pie' house; John Wilson, aka Christopher North, the sharp-tongued contributor to Blackwood's, stands as a statue, as does Adam Black, sometime publisher of the *Edinburgh Review*.

Greyfriars Kirkyard, Canongate Graveyard and Old Calton Burial Ground stand as different tributes entirely to past greats of the literary world. The pauper's grave of Robert Fergusson, later given a headstone by Robert Burns, lies with that of Adam Smith in Canongate Graveyard.

Pray Mr. Pattieson, have you been in EDINBURGH?" I answered in probably not so faithfully as I am doomed to do, through a narrow and passing by a HIGH and antique building with TURRETs and wo

4.

5.

Greyfriars is the final resting place of William Creech, Allan Ramsay and William Smellie, whilst David Hume, William Blackwood and Archibald Constable lie interred at Old Calton.

In a recent development, contemporary poets are celebrated in Edinburgh Park on the outskirts of the city. Twelve herms, or bronze heads, are on display, accompanied by a biographical note and poem. The public art programme also includes an award-winning poetry bus shelter.

Edinburgh: fuel for the creative mind

The true stories – and rumoured ones – of Edinburgh's colourful inhabitants have inspired writers for centuries. The built fabric, the urban landscape, the green spaces and the residents of the city are woven into many works.

James Hogg and Robert Louis Stevenson both wrote acclaimed novels whose central theme was duality. Deacon William Brodie was their inspiration. By day, he was a respected citizen, elected Deacon Councillor. But at night he was a gambler and a thief. His exposure following a failed robbery came as a great shock to the city. Brodie was hanged in Edinburgh on gallows he himself had designed as a master craftsman. Muriel Spark's heroine, Miss Jean Brodie, was created as a descendant of the Deacon and found herself torn between conflicting desires.

3. Allan Ramsay statue, Princes Street Gardens

4. Greyfriars Kirkyard, resting place of many key literary figures

5. Edinburgh Castle atop the Mound

rmative. "Then you must have passed, occasionally at least, though passage, leading out of the north-west corner of Parliament Square, 'es - Making good saying odd, Near the church and far from God.

No Sculpturd Marble here nor pompous lay
No Storied Urn nor animated Bust
This Simple Stone directs Pale Scotia's way
To pour her Sorrows o'er her Poets Dust

1.

2.

1. Calton Hill with its striking memorials
2. The epitaph to Robert Fergusson written by Robert Burns

Other grisly stories have inspired over the centuries. Robert Louis Stevenson's *The Body Snatcher* and Dylan Thomas's *The Doctor and the Devil* drew inspiration from the notorious duo of serial killers, Burke and Hare, who killed 15 people and then supplied their bodies for medical research.

The murder of Mary Queen of Scots' secretary and confidant David Rizzio at Holyrood stirred Rafael Sabatini to write *The Night of the Holyrood*, the creation of Algernon Swinburne's *Bothwell* and an opera, *Rizzio*, by Charles Dibdin.

The famous Porteous Riots of Edinburgh form the backdrop to one of Scotland's greatest novels, Walter Scott's *Heart of Midlothian*. The riot centred around Captain John Porteous who executed a popular young man for smuggling. During public protests at the execution he ordered his men to open fire, killing nine citizens. Though he was found guilty of murder, he was later reprieved, but lost his life to a furious mob that hanged him anyway.

A more poignant tale inspired the novel *Greyfriars Bobby* by Eleanor Atkinson, later made into a film by Disney. Bobby, a Skye terrier, was the faithful companion of a shepherd named Jock Gray who died in 1853 and was buried in Greyfriars Churchyard. The dog refused to leave his master's graveside until his own death 14 years later.

I WAS SEIZED WITH A KEEN DESIRE TO SEE HOLM
EAGERLY, WITH HIS HEAD SUNK UPON HIS CHEST, AN
HIS EVERY MOOD AND HABIT, HIS ATTITUDE AND M

4.

5.

It's not just the people of Edinburgh that have inspired – the city itself has impassioned writers. The twisted seams of Arthur's Seat and Salisbury Crags helped James Hutton explain his *Theory of the Earth* and provided the setting for many novels, from Scott's *Heart of Midlothian* to *The Lost World* of Arthur Conan Doyle. Mary Shelley set *Frankenstein* in the heart of Edinburgh, Charles Dickens praised it, and Ian Fleming sent James Bond to Fettes College after an indiscretion with a lady's maid at Eton. Another Edinburgh school, St Trinneans, inspired cartoonist Ronald Searle's series of books about a disreputable school for girls which in turn led to the classic British films of the 1950s.

The celebrated First World War poets Siegfried Sassoon and Wilfred Owen will forever be associated with Edinburgh's Craiglockhart Military Hospital, now part of the campus of Napier University. Their friendship at Craiglockhart led them to produce work that had a profound impact on English poetry.

Taverns and bars have always been a gathering place for literary figures. Whilst Burns favoured the Anchor Tavern, home of the Crochallan Fencibles drinking club, twentieth century figures such as Hugh MacDiarmid haunted Milnes Bar in Rose Street. And the true Edinburgh Detective John Rebus, the creation of Ian Rankin, made the Oxford Bar famous. Visitors to the city can learn a great deal about Edinburgh's literary life, and its bars, on The Scottish Literary Pub Tour, an entertaining introduction to writers connected with the city, from Burns to Irvine Welsh.

3. Robert Fergusson's grave in Canongate Kirkyard
4. St Giles Cathedral, with its stained glass window dedicated to Burns
5. Oxford Bar, Young Street, Edinburgh, haunt of Detective John Rebus

GAIN... ... HE WAS **PACING** THE ROOM **SWIFTLY,** S HANDS CLASPED BEHIND HIM. TO ME, WHO KNEW R TOLD THEIR OWN STORY. **HE WAS AT WORK AGAIN.**

Calton Hill, Edinburgh

Chapter 7. An international literary profile

Chapter 7
An international literary profile

Edinburgh's literary activities extend far beyond Scotland. International interest in classic Scottish literature continues to thrive, and there is also a keen and growing readership for contemporary Scottish writing.

BOSLIT, the Bibliography of Scottish Literature in Translation, has already recorded over 20,000 Scottish titles translated into over 100 languages worldwide. Contemporary Scottish works authored by Ian Rankin, Iain Banks, Alasdair Gray, Michel Faber and Louise Welsh have been translated into a range of languages from Czech to Catalan. Scottish publishers export almost a quarter of their total output overseas, demonstrating the international interest in books from Scotland.

As Scottish authors have been translated and disseminated widely across the world, foreign works have, in turn, been translated and brought to the attention of English-speaking audiences. Key among such translators is poet Alastair Reid. A son of the manse from Wigtown, he was a staff writer on the *New Yorker* magazine for many years. He has spent much of his life immersed in other cultures and languages and is the foremost translator of Latin American writers Pablo Neruda and Jorge Luis Borges.

The Scottish Publishers Association co-ordinates the activities of members in marketing their books overseas. The SPA also shares its expertise with publishing bodies all over the world. Delegations from these bodies regularly visit Scotland to learn from Scottish publishers; recent delegations coming from Sweden, China, Norway and Canada.

Glasgow est une ville magnifique, dit McAlp jamais? Parce que personne n'imagine vivre i utilisée par un artiste, même ses habitants r

2.   3.   4.

In turn, the Edinburgh International Book Festival attracts authors from over 20 countries and visitors from all over the world, and creates opportunities for authors to foster international connections. Bookcase, a joint venture with the British Council and Scottish Arts Council, introduces international literature event organisers to new Scottish and global writers and has led to readings in Colombia, Bulgaria, Brazil and Argentina.

Poetry, storytelling and education

'Minds fructify across generations and oceans, otherwise literature and art and music would be empty interludes and ornament' George Mackay Brown.

The Scottish Poetry Library has always aimed to place Scottish Poetry in an international context, representing many languages and countries in its collection. Recent events, workshops and readings have further strengthened global connections. The Japanese collection has recently been extended, and haiku workshops were run in primary schools as part of a Japanese festival; Northern Lights celebrated Norwegian poetry, featuring lament and laughter alike; EPIC (European Poetry Information Centre) links dozens of European Poetry websites; and the New Alliance project brought both French and American poets to Scotland to read and discuss their work.

1. Italian translation of *The Beach of Falesa* by Robert Louis Stevenson
2. Italian translation of *Acid House* by Irvine Welsh
3. Catalan translation of *Two Scottish Poets*
4. One of a series of postcards produced by the Scottish Poetry Library

urquoi est-ce qu'on ne le remarque presque ondit Thaw... Mais quand une ville n'a jamais été ent pas dans leur imaginaire.

The Scottish Storytelling Centre acts as an important channel for diverse world cultures as well as a celebration of Scotland's own traditions. Besides an annual festival in Edinburgh, events worldwide celebrate the tradition of the spoken story. Regular exchanges take place between Perm, Russia, and Scotland; 'Destination Viking' aims to link local and minority cultures across the northern hemisphere; and 'This Earth for Us' presented the tradition of telling stories in sand by women in southern Australia.

Intercultural relationships between Scotland and other countries are enriched through exchanges between schools. These range from friendship links between Edinburgh and Kenyan schools, to cultural exchanges with schools in Tanzania, Malawi and Madagascar. Closer to home, the EU Comenius Programme links several Edinburgh schools with schools across Europe in themed exchanges.

The Pushkin Prize, established in Scotland in 1987 by the great-great-grand-daughter of the Russian poet and writer Aleksandr Pushkin, encourages creative writing among young people in state schools throughout Scotland and in St Petersburg, Russia.

Initiatives such as these should provide the foundations of the exchanges of ideas, partnerships and understanding which Edinburgh UNESCO City of Literature seeks to promote.

Final words

Edinburgh: part of a global family

Edinburgh has made a remarkable contribution to literature and learning through its centuries of writing, publishing, reading and celebration of the written word, as this document testifies.

Scotland's capital city is eager to share the literary riches of its country and its contemporary literary culture too – the book festivals, the library resources and the sheer exuberance of 21st century literary life in Scotland.

The principal gesture that Edinburgh wishes to make, however, goes beyond those things. It centres on a wish to offer to other cities and other nations the hand of friendship in a particular way. We offer a simple model for nurturing the human achievement that derives from literature and the life around books.

This model is shaped against the outline of our own Scottish culture of the book. Yet it is also designed to be handed on – like a baton – and to fit comfortably with nations elsewhere, encouraging the ambition to be a world city of literature.

Scotland offers an idea for a global family of cities of literature: These will be cities that honour both the book and the people with a founding pledge based not on past success or present triumph but on two questions that invite a compact with future generations: what more can we do to deserve to be called "a city of literature" and how do we develop that idea for the benefit of our citizens and as an inspiration to other countries?

We can now turn another page in the world's story of the book with the foundation of friendships, new partnerships and covenants with the future through world cities of literature.

James Boyle
Chairman, Edinburgh UNESCO City of Literature
June 2004

Overleaf:
Double trouble – sharing a love of reading

Acknowledgements

Acknowledgements
Edinburgh UNESCO City of Literature

Funders

Management Team
James Boyle (Chairman)
Lorraine Fannin, Director, Scottish Publishers Association
Catherine Lockerbie, Director, Edinburgh International Book Festival
Martyn Wade, National Librarian, National Library of Scotland

Steering Committee
Professor Ian Campbell, University of Edinburgh
Sheila Cannell, Director of Library Services, University of Edinburgh
Karen Cunningham, Head of Libraries, Information & Learning, Glasgow
    City Council
Dr Linda Dryden, Napier University
June Edgar, Creative Industries Manager, Scottish Enterprise Edinburgh
    and Lothian
David Graham, Managing Director, Canongate Books
Marc Lambert, Chief Executive, Scottish Book Trust
Stuart MacDonald, Head of Sport and Co-ordination Division, Scottish Executive
Robyn Marsack, Director, Scottish Poetry Library
Matthew Perren, Manager, George St Edinburgh branch, Ottakar's Booksellers
Ian Rankin, Writer
Donald Smith, Director, The Netherbow: Scottish Storytelling Centre
Bill Wallace, Head of Libraries and Information Services,
    City of Edinburgh Council
Dr Gavin Wallace, Head of Literature, Scottish Arts Council

Staff
Jenny Brown, Project Manager
Inez Forbes, Administrator

Picture Research
Fiona Morrison Graham

Consultant
Rachel Blanche

Production Adviser
Ron Grosset, Geddes & Grosset, book publishers

Contact
Edinburgh UNESCO City of Literature
Scottish Book Centre
137 Dundee Street, Edinburgh EH11 1BG
T +44 (0) 131 229 9498
E edinburgh@cityofliterature.com W www.cityofliterature.com

Edinburgh UNESCO City of Literature Trust is a company limited by guarantee
and not having a share capital. Registered in Scotland SC270581.
Registered as a charity in Scotland no. SCO035697. Registered Office 137 Dundee
Street, Edinburgh EH11 1BG.

Publicity
Colman Getty PR
20 Forth Street, Edinburgh EH1 3LH
T +44 (0) 131 477 7950
E Scotland@colmangettypr.co.uk

Source of quotes

Grateful acknowledgement is made to the following sources for permission to reproduce material in this book previously published elsewhere. Every effort has been made to trace copyright holders, but if any have been inadvertently overlooked, the publisher will be pleased to make the necessary arrangements at the first opportunity.

Chapter 1

Page 2/3
From *Strip Jack Naked* by Ian Rankin, published by Orion Books 1992.

Page 4/5
From *The No 1. Ladies' Detective Agency* by Alexander McCall Smith, published by Polygon 1998.

Page 6/7
From *The Prime of Miss Jean Brodie* by Muriel Spark, published by Penguin Books 1961.

Page 8/9
From *The Thirty-Nine Steps* by John Buchan, published by William Blackwood and Sons 1915.

Page 10/11
From *Treasure Island* by Robert Louis Stevenson, published by Cassell 1883.

Page 14/15
From *Confessions of a Justified Sinner* by James Hogg, 1824.

Page 18/19
From *Auld Reekie* by Robert Fergusson, written between 1771 and 1774.

Page 20/21
From *The Brus* by John Barbour, c.1375

Page 21/22
From *Peter Pan* by J.M. Barrie (1860-1937)

Chapter 2

Page 26/27
From *A Treatise on Human Nature* by David Hume (1739-40)

Page 28/9
From *Inquiry into the Human Mind* by Thomas Reid, 1764

Page 30/31
Benjamin Franklin (1706-1790) on his trip to Edinburgh, 1759

Chapter 3

Page 34/35
From the 'History of Publishing' Encyclopaedia Britannica, Encyclopaedia Britannica Premium Service
http://www.britannica.com/eb/article?eu=117358

Page 36/37
From *The Secret Chamber* (Dedicated to the inquirers in the Norman Tower) by Margaret Oliphant.
From *Blackwood's Edinburgh Magazine* (1876, Dec)

Page 38/39
From *Life Of Pi* by Yann Martel, first published in Great Britain by Canongate Books, 2002

Chapter 4

Page 42/43
From *A Man's A Man For A' That*, Robert Burns (1759-1796)

Page 44/45
From *Harry Potter and the Chamber of Secrets* by J.K. Rowling published by Bloomsbury 1998.

Page 46/47
Scottish Stones by Fabio Milazzo, from Poet Makar Bard 2001-2003: a collection of poems by young
people written at the Scottish Poetry Library, 2003

Chapter 5

Page 50/51
From *Aunt Julia*, one of the *Collected Poems* by Norman MacCaig published by Chatto & Windus. Used
by permission of The Random House Group Limited.

Page 54/55
From *Hallaig* a poem by Sorley MacLean, reproduced in *From Wood to Ridge* published by
Carcanet, 1989

Chapter 6

Page 60/61
From *The Heart of Midlothian* by Walter Scott, 1819.

Page 62/63
From *Scandal in Bohemia* by Sir Arthur Conan-Doyle, 1891.

Chapter 7

Page 66/67
From *Lanark: a life in four books* by Alasdair Gray, first published in 1981 in Great Britain by Canongate
Books, 14 High Street, Edinburgh, EH1 1TE

Acknowledgements

End papers:
The Dance of Dun-Can, from Boswell's, *The Journal of a Tour to the Hebrides*, 1785, illustrated by Thomas Rowlandson. Courtesy of the Trustees of the National Library of Scotland.

Page i:
Dugald Stewart Monument, Calton Hill, Edinburgh. Courtesy of The City of Edinburgh Council.

Page iv:
J.K. Rowling, author, by Richard Young.

Page 3:
1. *Peter Pan* by Mabel Lucie Attwell. Courtesy of the Mabel Lucie Attwell Estate.
2. Iain Banks, author, reading to children at the Edinburgh International Book Festival. Courtesy of the Scottish Arts Council.
3. Candia McWilliam, author. Courtesy of Bloomsbury Publishing.
4. Irvine Welsh, author, by Iain McIntosh.

Page 4:
1. Masthead illustration of *44 Scotland Street*, by Alexander McCall Smith, illustrated by Iain McIntosh.
2. *The No. 1 Ladies' Detective Agency*, by Alexander McCall Smith, published by Polygon.
3. Alexander McCall Smith, author. Courtesy of the Edinburgh International Book Festival.
4. *Perfect Days* by Liz Lochhead, photographed by Euan Myles. Courtesy of the Traverse Theatre, Edinburgh.
5. Detail from *Poets' Pub* by Alexander Moffat, 1980, showing Edwin Morgan, author. Courtesy of the Scottish National Portrait Gallery. ©The Artist

Page 5:
6. James Kelman, author, by Douglas Robertson. Courtesy of Secker & Warburg Publishers, 1994.
7. *How Late It Was, How Late* by James Kelman, illustrated by Colum Leith. Courtesy of Secker & Warburg Publishers, 1994.
8. *Lanark: A Life in Four Books* by Alasdair Gray, first published in 1981 in Great Britain by Canongate Books Ltd.

9. *Lanark: A Life in Four Books* by Alasdair Gray. Artwork for the first edition of Lanark by Alasdair Gray. Published by Canongate Books Ltd in 1981. Courtesy of the National Library of Scotland.

Page 6:
1. Dorothy Dunnett, author, by Alison Dunnett.
2. *Gemini* by Dorothy Dunnett, illustrated by Nicky Palin. Courtesy of Penguin Books.
3. *The Prime of Miss Jean Brodie* by Muriel Spark. Courtesy of Penguin Books.

Page 7:
4. Muriel Spark, author. Courtesy of the Trustees of the National Library of Scotland.
5. Neil M. Gunn, author. Courtesy of the Trustees of the National Library of Scotland and Lt. Commander Diarmid Gunn.
6. *Sunset Song* by Lewis Grassic Gibbon, illustrated by John Bulloch Souter. Courtesy of Canongate Books Ltd.
7. *Highland River* by Neil M. Gunn, illustrated by Bert White. Courtesy of Canongate Books Ltd.
8. *The Serpent* by Neil M. Gunn, illustrated by D.Y. Cameron. Courtesy of Canongate Books Ltd.

Page 8:
1. Robert Garioch, poet, by Gordon Wright.
2. Sir Compton Mackenzie, author, by Robert H. Westwater, 1962. Courtesy of the Scottish National Portrait Gallery. ©The Estate of Robert Heriot Westwater.
3. Catherine Carswell, author. Courtesy of the Trustees of the National Library of Scotland.
4. John Buchan, author. Courtesy of the Trustees of the National Library of Scotland.
5. The one-shilling bookstall edition of *The Thirty-Nine Steps* by John Buchan, published by William Blackwood. Courtesy of the Trustees of the National Library of Scotland.

Page 9:

6. Sorley MacLean, author, by Cailean MacLean.
7. *Poets' Pub* by Alexander Moffat, 1980. Courtesy of the Scottish National Portrait Gallery. ©The Artist.
8. Hugh MacDiarmid (C.M. Grieve), by Robert H. Westwater, 1962. Courtesy of the Scottish National Portrait Gallery. ©The Estate of Robert Heriot Westwater.
9. Norman MacCaig, poet, by Robin Gillanders.

Page 10:

1. *Holy Willie's Prayer* by Robert Burns. Courtesy of University of Edinburgh.
2. Robert Burns, poet, by Alexander Nasmyth, 1787. Courtesy of the Scottish National Portrait Gallery.
3. Helen Cruickshank, poet. Courtesy of the Trustees of the National Library of Scotland.
4. Robert Louis Stevenson, author, by Count Girolamo Nerli, 1892. Courtesy of the Scottish National Portrait Gallery.

Page 11:

5. *The Strange Case of Dr. Jekyll and Mr. Hyde* by Robert Louis Stevenson. Courtesy of the Trustees of the National Library of Scotland.
6. French translation of *Treasure Island* by Robert Louis Stevenson, published by Collection Hetzel, Paris, 1885. Courtesy of the Bibliography of Scottish Literature in Translation (BOSLIT).
7. *Kidnapped* by Robert Louis Stevenson. Courtesy of the Trustees of the National Library of Scotland.
8. Sir Walter Scott in his study, Castle Street, Edinburgh, engraved by Robert Charles Bell after the portrait by John Watson Gordon, c. 1850. Courtesy of University of Edinburgh.
9. Loch Katrine looking towards Ellen's Isle, illustrated by Thomas Allom, from *Scotland Illustrated* vol. II.

Page 12:

Scott Monument, Princes Street Gardens, Edinburgh, photographed by Ross Gillespie and Tricia Malley. Courtesy of broad daylight ltd.

Page 14:

1. *The Private Memoirs and Confessions of a Justified Sinner* by James Hogg. Courtesy of the Trustees of the National Library of Scotland.
2. Tobias Smollett, author. Courtesy of the National Portrait Gallery, London.
3. James Hogg, author. Courtesy of University of Edinburgh.
4. John Home, author. Courtesy of University of Edinburgh.

Page 15:

5. *The Douglas* by John Home. Courtesy of the Trustees of the National Library of Scotland.
6. Susan Edmonstone Ferrier, author, by Augustin Edouart. Courtesy of the Scottish National Portrait Gallery.
7. Margaret Oliphant, author, by Janet Mary Oliphant. Courtesy of the Scottish National Portrait Gallery.

Page 16/17:

Manuscript of *Zaidee: A Romance*, published in *Blackwood's Magazine*, 1854 -1855 by Margaret Oliphant. Courtesy of the Trustees of the National Library of Scotland.

Page 18:

1. Arthur Conan Doyle, author. Courtesy of University of Edinburgh.
2. *Sherlock Holmes* box set. Binder design by David Eccles. Published by The Folio Society, 1994.
3. Statue of Allan Ramsay, Princes Street Gardens, Edinburgh, by Inez Forbes.
4. Illustration from *Holiday House* by Catherine Sinclair. Courtesy of the Trustees of the National Library of Scotland.

Page 19:

5. James Thomson, composer and poet. Courtesy of the Scottish National Portrait Gallery.
6. *Rule Britannia*, score and words by James Thomson. Courtesy of the Trustees of the National Library of Scotland.
7. *Ossian*, translated by James Macpherson (with the armorial stamp of Napoleon's Library at Fontainebleau). Courtesy of the Trustees of the National Library of Scotland.
8. Robert Fergusson, poet, by Alexander Runciman. Courtesy of the Scottish National Portrait Gallery.

9. Grave of Robert Fergusson, Canongate Kirkyard, Edinburgh, by Roderick Graham.

Page 20:
1. Manuscript of *The Brus* by John Barbour. Courtesy of the Trustees of the National Library of Scotland.
2. King James I of Scotland and his wife, illustration from the Forman Armorial. Courtesy of the Trustees of the National Library of Scotland.
3. The manuscript of *The Kingis Quair* by King James I. Courtesy of the Bodleian Library, Oxford.

Page 21:
4. Poems by William Dunbar, printed by Chepman and Myllar, Edinburgh. Courtesy of the Trustees of the National Library of Scotland.
5. Extract from the manuscript of *The New Testament in Scots* by William Lorimer. Courtesy of the Trustees of the National Library of Scotland.

Page 22:
1. A young boy discovering Harry Potter through Braille with J.K. Rowling, author. Courtesy of the Royal Blind Asylum and School, Edinburgh.
2. *Harry Potter and the Philosopher's Stone* by J.K. Rowling, illustrated by Thomas Taylor. Courtesy of Bloomsbury Publishing.
3. Dutch translation of *Harry Potter* titles by J.K.Rowling, illustrated by Ien van Laanen, Amsterdam. Graphic design by Anne Lammers, Amsterdam.

Page 23:
4. *Peter Pan in Kensington Gardens* by J.M. Barrie, illustrated by Arthur Rackham, published by Hodder and Stoughton. Courtesy of the Arthur Rackham Estate.
5. *Wind in the Willows* by Kenneth Grahame. Courtesy of the Trustees of the National Library of Scotland.
6. J.M. Barrie, author, by Sir William Nicholson, 1904. Courtesy of the Scottish National Portrait Gallery.
7. *A Child's Garden of Verses* by Robert Louis Stevenson. Courtesy of the Trustees of the National Library of Scotland.

Page 24:
Peter Pan and Wendy by J.M. Barrie. Courtesy of the Trustees of the National Library of Scotland.

Page 27:
1. Robert Burns, poet, by Alexander Nasmyth, 1828. Courtesy of the Scottish National Portrait Gallery.
2. David Hume, historian and philosopher, by Allan Ramsay, 1766. Courtesy of University of Edinburgh.
3. Lord Kames, historian, by David Martin, 1794. Courtesy of the Scottish National Portrait Gallery.
4. Adam Ferguson, historian, by Sir Joshua Reynolds. Courtesy of the Scottish National Portrait Gallery.
5. Adam Smith, philosopher, by an unknown artist. Courtesy of the Scottish National Portrait Gallery.

Page 28:
1. German translation of *A Treatise of Human Nature* by David Hume. Courtesy of the Trustees of the National Library of Scotland.
2. *A Treatise of Human Nature* by David Hume. Courtesy of the Trustees of the National Library of Scotland.
3. Salisbury Crags, from Grant's *Old and New Edinburgh*.

Page 29:
4. Dugald Stewart, philosopher. Courtesy of University of Edinburgh.
5. Swedish translation of *Essay on the History of Civil Society* by Adam Ferguson. Courtesy of the Trustees of the National Library of Scotland.
6. *An Inquiry into the Human Mind* by Thomas Reid. Courtesy of the Trustees of the National Library of Scotland.
7. Swedish translation of *History of America* by William Robertson. Courtesy of the Trustees of the National Library of Scotland.
8. William Robertson, historian and principal of Edinburgh University, by Sir Henry Raeburn. Courtesy of University of Edinburgh.

Page 30:
1. Thomas Carlyle, historian, by John Linnell, 1844. Courtesy of the Scottish National Portrait Gallery.
2. *Blackwood's Magazine*, 1882 edition. Courtesy of the Trustees of the National Library of Scotland.

3. John Wilson (Christopher North), Professor of Moral Philosophy. Courtesy of University of Edinburgh.
4. Robert Burns, poet, by Alexander Reid, 1795/6. Courtesy of the Scottish National Portrait Gallery.
5. Henry Mackenzie, author, by Colvin Smith, c.1827. Courtesy of the Scottish National Portrait Gallery.

Page 31:
6. Thistle emblem of the *Encyclopaedia Britannica*. Courtesy of the Trustees of the National Library of Scotland.
7. *The Man of Feeling* by Henry Mackenzie. Courtesy of the Trustees of the National Library of Scotland.
8. *The Birds of America*, illustrated by John James Audubon. Courtesy of the National Museums of Scotland.

Page 32:
David Hume, historian and philosopher, by Louis Carrogis. Courtesy of the Scottish National Portrait Gallery.

Page 35:
1. Thomas Nelson & Sons colophon, 1798. Courtesy of the Trustees of the National Library of Scotland.
2. William Creech, publisher, by Sir Henry Raeburn, 1806. Courtesy of the Scottiah National Portrait Gallery.
3. Androw Myllar's printer's device. Courtesy of the Trustees of the National Library of Scotland.
4. Archibald Constable, publisher, by Andrew Geddes, 1813. Courtesy of the Scottish National Portrait Gallery.
5. Frontispiece of *Waverley* from *The Waverley Novels*, by Sir Walter Scott. Courtesy of the Trustees of the National Library of Scotland.

Page 36:
1. Francis Jeffrey, one of the Lords of Session, by Sir G. Hayter. Courtesy of University of Edinburgh.
2. John Murray I, publisher. Courtesy of the John Murray Archive, London.
3. David Livingstone, missionary and explorer, by Joseph Brown. Courtesy of the John Murray Archive, London.

4. 'The missionary escapes from the lion.' From *Missionary Travels and Researches in South Africa* by David Livingstone, published by John Murray, London 1857. Courtesy of the Trustees of the National Library of Scotland.

Page 37:

5. Thomas De Quincey, author, by Sir John Watson Gordon, 1846. Courtesy of the Scottish National Portrait Gallery.

6. Oscar Wilde, author and playwright, in New York, 1882, by N. Sarony. Courtesy of the National Portrait Gallery, London.

7. Thomas Carlyle, historian, by Mrs Helen Allingham, 1879. Courtesy of the Scottish National Portrait Gallery.

8. John Gibson Lockhart, author and son-in-law of Sir Walter Scott, by Sir Francis Grant. Courtesy of the Scottish National Portrait Gallery.

Page 38:

1. Flat hemisphere map from Philips *Modern School Atlas*, London: George Philip, 1935. Courtesy of the Trustees of the National Library of Scotland.

Page 39:

2. *Chambers Pocket Dictionary*, published by Chambers, Edinburgh.

3. *The Full Cupboard of Life* by Alexander McCall Smith, published by Polygon.

4. *A Highland Lady in France* by Elizabeth Grant of Rothiemurchus, published by Tuckwell Press.

5. *Sun Circle* by Neil M. Gunn, illustrated detail by Nicholas Roerich. Courtesy of Canongate Books Ltd.

6. *Directory of Publishing in Scotland, 2004/5*, photographed by Graham Clark. Published by Scottish Publishers Association, 2004.

Page 40:

Life of Pi by Yann Martel, painting by Andy Bridge. First published in Great Britain by Canongate Books Ltd.

Page 43:

1. Statue of John Knox in the quadrangle of New College, Edinburgh. Taken from *John Knox, Democrat* by Roderick Graham, published by Hale.

2. Dr. Thomas Guthrie's Ragged Classroom, Edinburgh. Courtesy of the National Archives of Scotland.

3. Allan Ramsay Senior, poet, by William Aikman, 1722. Courtesy of the Scottish National Portrait Gallery.

4. Dr. Samuel Johnson and James Boswell on the High Street in Edinburgh from Boswell's, *The Journal of A Tour to the Hebrides*, illustrated by Thomas Rowlandson. Courtesy of the Trustees of the National Library of Scotland.

Page 44:

1. Craighouse at Napier University, Edinburgh. Courtesy of Napier University.

2. Heriot-Watt University, Edinburgh. Courtesy of Heriot-Watt University.

3. Matthew Taylor, smallest reader meets largest book, photographed by Mark K. Jackson. First published in *Quarto*, by the National Library of Scotland.

Page 45:

4. Amu storytelling at the Edinburgh International Book Festival. Courtesy of the Edinburgh International Book Festival.

5/6. Reading at the Edinburgh International Book Festival. Courtesy of the Edinburgh International Book Festival.

Page 46:

1. At the Edinburgh International Book Festival book sale. Courtesy of the Edinburgh International Book Festival.

2/4. Postcard produced by the Scottish Poetry Library.

3. Reading on the lawn at the Edinburgh International Book Festival. Courtesy of the Edinburgh International Book Festival.

Page 47:

5. Story writing at the Edinburgh International Book Festival. Courtesy of the Edinburgh International Book Festival.

6. Poem written by members of Black Community Development Project over 10's group and postcard produced by the Scottish Poetry Library, from *Pencils, Pixels and Poems*, artist Catriona Grant.

7. Postcard produced by Tweed Rivers Interpretation Project, photographed by James Carter.

Page 48:

Poster for the third Edinburgh Book Festival by Michael Foreman.

Page 51:

The Great Book of Gaelic. Published by Canongate Books Ltd.

Page 53:
Celtic border: Poem Anon c. 1200, taken from *The Great Book of Gaelic*, illustrated by Alasdair Gray. Published by Canongate Books Ltd.

Page 54:
1. Entry from the *Illustrated Gaelic-English Dictionary* by Edward Dwelly. Published by Birlinn.
2. George Campbell Hay, author, illustrated by Gerald Mayor. Courtesy of the Trustees of the National Library of Scotland.
3. *Ath-Aithne* by Martin MacIntyre. Published by CLAR, June 2004.
4. *Tocasaid 'Ain Tuirc* by Duncan Gillies. Published by CLAR, June 2004.
5. *An Oidhche Mus Do Sheol Sinn* by Angus Peter. Published by CLAR, October 2003.

Page 55:
6. *Gath* magazine. Published by GATH Publications, 2003.
7. *King O' the Midden, Manky Mingin Rhymes in Scots*, illustrated by Bob Dewar. Published by Itchy Coo, 2003.
8. *A Scots Dialect Dictionary* compiled by Alexander Warrack, M.A. Published by W & R Chambers Ltd, Edinburgh, 1911.
9. The Daunce of the Sevin Deidly Sinnis, from the *Pocket Book of Scottish Quotations* by David Ross. Published by Birlinn.

Page 57:
Hugh MacDiarmid memorial at Langholm, sculpted by Jake Harvey. Courtesy of David Morrison/Dumfries & Galloway Tourist Board.

Page 58:
Statue of Greyfriars Bobby, Edinburgh, by Colin Baxter. Courtesy of Colin Baxter Photography.

Pages 60-61:
1. Palace of Holyroodhouse
2. Walter Scott monument
3. Statue of Allan Ramsay
4. Greyfriars Kirkyard
5. Edinburgh Castle, all illustrated by Iain McIntosh.

Pages 62-63:

1. Calton Hill
2. Epitaph on Robert Fergusson's grave
3. Robert Fergusson's grave
4. St Giles Cathedral
5. The Oxford Bar, all illustrated by Iain McIntosh.

Pages 64:

6. Calton Hill, illustrated by Iain McIntosh.

Page 67:

1. Italian translation of *The Beach of Falesá* by Robert Louis Stevenson, illustrated by Paul Gauguin, published by Passigli Editori. Courtesy of the Bibliography of Scottish Literature in Translation (BOSLIT).
2. Italian translation of *Acid House* by Irvine Welsh, illustrated by Robert Clifford, published by Ugo Guanda Editore in Parma. Courtesy of the Bibliography of Scottish Literature in Translation (BOSLIT).
3. Catalan translation of *Stewart Conn and Anna Crowe: Two Scottish Poets on La Mola*, illustrated by Francesc Davi, published by Castellar del Valles, 2002. Courtesy of the Bibliography of Scottish Literature in Translation (BOSLIT).
4. Postcard produced by the Scottish Poetry Library.

Page 72:

Double trouble, Davy and Tommy Zyw sharing the love of reading, Edinburgh. Courtesy of Readiscovery Campaign, 1995.